THE PAPER TRAIL

THE PAPER TRAIL

The Real Estate Professional's Guide to Documented Liability Protection and Marketing Success

Revised Edition

Oliver E. Frascona

Risk Reduction Series
from Real Law Books, Inc.

Library of Congress Cataloging in Publication Data
Frascona, Oliver E., 1947—
  The paper trail.

  (Risk Reduction Series)
  Appendix
  1. Real estate business—Records and correspondence. 2. Real estate agents—Malpractice. 3. Real estate business—Law and legislation. I. Title. II. Series. HD1386.5.F7 1987   333.33'068   89-24349
ISBN 0-941937-01-1 (pbk.)

Printed in the United States of America

Risk Reduction Series

from

Real Law Books, Inc.
Post Office Box 3113
Boulder, Colorado 80307-3113
U.S.A.

Acknowledgments

This book is dedicated to the professional real estate people who assist us all in the search for, acquisition of, financing of, and sale of real estate, one of the most precious physical commodities available in our free society, and to the National Association of Realtors® which, through the never-ending efforts of its members, works tirelessly to preserve the rights of each of us to buy, own, use, and sell real estate, and to their continuing efforts and commitment to educate Realtors®, the public, and governments large and small about the ever-changing aspects of private property ownership.

It is most appropriate to pause to thank all those people, real estate professionals, brokers and salespeople alike, executive officers, clients and friends, in and out of the real estate profession, who have encouraged this effort and did not let me put it aside. The help and encouragement given by these friends, my family, and my editor are what have made the difference. To those who recognize some of the facts and wording, thank you for letting me use your real-life experiences. As you can see I have changed the names to protect you all.

You are the people who make the world go around and to you this book is dedicated.

Preface

Man is the only animal on earth that is born without knowledge. All other animals seem to be born knowing most of what they will need to exist. As each of us goes through life, we observe what others do, as well as what we ourselves do, and we compare these actions or inactions against some internal standard of correctness. The result we describe as our success or failure. From repeating this exercise every day, we learn what we feel it takes to be successful.

I have had the opportunity over the last decade—as a participant, a real estate broker, and as an attorney—to review a wide variety of real estate transactions. I finally decided that if I would take the time, could suffer the feeling of not having included everything or of having written some part in a manner I would later wish was different, to write down the hindsight of some of my experiences, the result could be useful to people as a place to start, a sort of guide, for helping them step around many of the trouble spots I have encountered. My thought has been that a book describing the preparation of written correspondence, disclaimers and notices, based on the actual experiences that I have enjoyed or endured, would function like a good assistant in a wide variety of real estate transactions.

This book is an attempt to give you, as a real estate professional, an observation point from which to map your own descriptive correspondence. Use it to take the high ground. Just as we find it natural to observe others in order to learn and progress, use the observations in this book and its model cases to sight your way to more successful transactions. It will help you eliminate the ever-pressing sensation of needing to look backwards over your shoulder for disputes, confrontation, and litigation. Look instead over its shoulder in strengthening your own internal standard of correctness and communication. It is the strength of your own standard, properly imparted to those with whom you transact business, which will ultimately determine your success in dealing with people.

Laying your own "paper trail" will help you fully inform others of the alternatives presented, tighten your contract preparation, improve your decision-making skills, and reduce your liability. Your success there, in turn, will arise from your increased ease and efficiency in stating clearly to everyone—your clients and customers, lenders, the public, suppliers, and others on whom we all rely for support and business—the pertinent facts of any deal, the limits of your liability, and the necessary notifications and confirmations.

Caveat

This material is designed to give the reader as many "places to start" as possible. It is hoped that it will stimulate the reader to design and implement a set of standard forms for the disclosure of information and the updating of letters sent to various parties. Although great care has been taken to insure that the information contained is accurate, pertinent, and to the point, each situation and each intended use is different. All letters and disclaimers should be the work product of the reader as an individual author. While written for general use in Colorado and throughout the United States, the reader should utilize competent local legal advice before modifying and utilizing any of the material contained herein.

This publication is sold with the understanding that neither the author nor the law firm of which he is a member is giving legal or other professional advice nor recommending the use of these letters or other material in the form in which they appear in this book. This publication is not and should not be used as a substitute for legal advice.

The author makes no representations as to the accuracy of the information contained herein and is not liable to anyone for its use or misuse. This is a copyrighted work and is not to be photocopied or reproduced in any manner without the prior express written consent of the author. The price has been kept low to encourage everyone to have a personal copy that can contain their own notes and modifications. Use this publication and the material contained herein at your own risk. THERE ARE NO WARRANTIES, EXPRESS OR IMPLIED, INCLUDING FITNESS FOR A PARTICULAR PURPOSE, MADE WITH RESPECT TO THIS MATERIAL.

Although I have used the names of friends and associates, that should not be interpreted as an endorsement or disparagement. Cases in point are just that, actual cases. The names have been changed in some cases to protect us all.

Table of Contents

Chapter Two
Obtaining the Listing 23

Introduction

To be helpful, the book had to have a structure. I have chosen the pattern of events in the "normal" real estate transaction, if there still is such a thing. My hope is that the information and ideas contained in this book will spark your thought process and give you an idea base from which to work. From that base you can always create a polite and clear note or letter which meets your need to disclose information to your clients and customers, disclaim liability for actions that were never yours to start with, and answers questions for the record. It's simple. It's a good habit. And you will see how the use of professional correspondence not only protects you and your broker but also consistently helps you sell real estate.

You know that as a modern real estate professional you deal with, and come to literally depend upon, numerous different members of the public at large. You say many things to various clients, customers, subagents, agents for other parties, lenders, title companies, inspectors, appraisers, investors and other people. You often make these statements intending to encourage or induce someone to take a particular action, purchase, sell, finance, lease, appraise or otherwise deal with real property. In addition, as a cautious professional, you are becoming more and more aware of the duty being imposed upon real estate professionals by brokers, lenders, other agents, regulatory authorities, boards, legislatures, and courts to disclose ever-increasing amounts of information. Often the standard by which you might be judged is not even available for inspection until the authority actually decides the case.

Even clear, concise, consistent speech has always been susceptible to various interpretations at the time it is uttered. Later, the memory tends to remember what one wants it to remember. The golden rule of "the test of a communication is what the addressee can reasonably be expected to understand" is being stretched to the limit. The court system, the regulators, the legislatures at all levels, in an effort to protect us all from even ourselves, are increasing the amount of regulation to be imposed on the business of providing access to shelter, the most basic of all brokerage businesses.

Carefully drafted contracts alone, while always a necessity for the real estate professional, are no longer enough. Cover letters, clarifying nearly all information presented and the extent of the broker's and agent's roles, are becoming a must. In the face of such potential liability, there is no need for the real estate professional to simply give up and write letters that will discourage the reader when the skillful use of the cover letter can also be a professional selling tool.

There are still buyers and sellers who want to and will consummate transactions through the brokerage network. In fact, it is the very complexity that we all abhor that is entrenching the real estate broker as a necessity in modern life. When I was an active broker it was far simpler. All loans were thirty-years fixed; governments did not have planned unit developments (PUD's); down-zoning was unknown; the approval process took three to four weeks; land available for development was plentiful; the air was clean; water, electricity and natural gas were everywhere. Not so today.

The skillful creation of a "paper trail," one that not only imparts a feeling of respect for the real estate professional in the eyes of the reader, but also fully informs, assists in reinforcing the sale, and presents vital information in a hard-to-dispute form, is the core of this work. It is my desire, then, that you take heart from this book, being confident in its use that you, too, can draft letters which will accomplish all this in your own situations.

Comments and sample letters are just that: samples. You should rethink your actual letter content—as well as the timeliness of sending various letters—and not rely solely on the forms I am presenting. Although each case is a little different, try to develop your own standard letters and habits so that you always handle the same situation in the same manner. Careful, planned consistency is the best defense. Establish yourself as a consistent professional.

You will find several related items included in one letter to save having to use the introduction again and again. This is not to suggest that all the information be included in a single letter. Several different approaches are included so that you can mix and match those items that are best for you. The information and presentation vary from letter to letter to give you a different approach to similar styles. In that way you will be able to tailor your letters to your own needs and be exposed to as many different ways of presenting information as possible. To save needless repetition, alternate paragraphs may appear under the same address. Some alternate clauses or explanations are located inside brackets [ ].

Recognizing that both sexes are actively represented in the real estate profession, I have tried to write so that the need to use a particular gender is eliminated. When that is not possible, I have used various genders at random. The use of any particular gender is to save the constant use of his/her, he/she.

Oliver E. Frascona

Chapter One

Helpful Professional Practices

The Ten Commandments of a Professional Agent

1. I will do my best to follow the letter and the spirit of the Code of Ethics established by the National Association of Realtors®.

2. I will keep everyone with whom I deal, including my broker, informed about every aspect of every transaction, promptly and in a business-like manner. I will always be a source of information, not a decision maker, for my clients and customers.

3. As a broker, I will always be available and accessible to assist and supervise all the agents who are under my control and to teach by example.

4. I will keep accurate and timely records of every aspect of all transactions in which I am involved.

5. I will not deal in securities or property management without the prior written consent of my broker.

6. I will conduct all my business as though it were to be reviewed by the Real Estate Commission on a daily basis.

7. I will conduct my personal life so as to augment the professional standing of my real estate company and associates.

8. I will never accept compensation for any service unless there is a written agreement, approved by my broker, covering such compensation.

9. Although I will endeavor to serve the public, I will always ask myself these questions:
   - "Is there someone more competent than I to answer this question, provide the requested or required information?"
   - "If I am not getting paid for this, is it perhaps because I should not be doing it?"
   - "Why am I giving advice?"

10. Without the prior written consent of my broker, I will not:
    - Serve as the attorney-in-fact for anyone.
    - Act in an agency capacity for anyone other than as provided in a written listing agreement approved by the company.
    - Accept a position as an escrow agent.
    - Obligate myself or the company.
    - Become a party to any contract.
    - Guarantee the performance of any party.

The Four D's of the Professional Agent

1. DECIDE whom you are going to represent:
   a. BEFORE you start representing anyone
   b. BEFORE someone thinks you are her agent
   c. CONSIDER the ramifications of representing:
      i.   The seller
      ii. The buyer
      iii. Both buyer and seller
      iv. Everyone involved

2. DISCLOSE your agency status to everyone:
   a. Your broker

b. Potential principals (other selling brokers)
c. Buyers
d. Lenders, appraisers, inspectors (third parties)

3. DOCUMENT your agency status by:
    a. Writing a letter to everyone
    b. Indicating it in the contract
    c. Sending an additional copy in other correspondence

4. DO as you have indicated:
    a. CONDUCT must equal REPRESENTATION
    b. CONDUCT overrides paperwork

The Real Estate Broker in Litigation

Seller and Broker Beware

The old days of "buyer beware" are gone. In their place has come an increasing attempt by the courts to "protect" the consumer from everyone, including, on occasion, himself. In this age of consumerism, everyone dealing with the public is coming under a great deal of scrutiny. Doctors, lawyers, manufacturers, distributors, retailers and real estate brokers all deal with and provide vital services to the public. The real estate broker is poised in a unique position as the purveyor of one of our most basic needs: shelter. In addition, the real estate professional has over the last decade made a successful effort to enhance the image of real estate brokers. The public and the court have accepted real estate salespeople as professionals, are treating them as such, and are holding them to expectations of top professional practices.

No Inflation and Greater Complexity

These are the two final nails in the unprepared broker's coffin. First, there is no consistent inflationary blanket to cover the mistakes of the past. Instead of just selling mistakes, everyone is having to live with them. Second, the world of real estate has gotten complicated. The analysis of the available financing from institutions nearly takes a degree in mathematics and the proficient use of a sophisticated calculator, not to mention a crystal ball for each new tax code revision. I am becoming a follower of the theory that tax code revisions are just an ongoing part of the "CPA Full Employment and Guaranteed Retirement Act."

Being secure about the type and extent of any financing that may be carried by the seller and anticipating the potential remedies of the various parties in the event of default require a law degree with a specialty in real estate law. The overlapping rules, including all the association, local, county, state and federal statutes and regulations, are increasing at a rate faster than anyone can even read. These often conflicting requirements place brokers in the middle of the political arena and leave them vulnerable to lawsuits from all sides.

The Demands Upon The Modern Professional Broker

The sale and acquisition of real estate has become so complicated that an untrained person, even one who is a professional in another field, is no longer able to navigate the safe route to a properly closed deal without a real estate professional as a guide. Into this world steps the real estate professional and her broker, the broker being liable not only for everything that she herself does but also for the acts of her agents.

The court, in an attempt to protect the public, often as not from itself, is placing more and more responsibilities on the broker and winding the fiduciary duty knot tighter and tighter. Brokers are increasingly being held responsible for their actions, inactions, contract drafting, and other responsibilities related to a real estate transaction. They must learn now how to generate sophisticated paperwork to document the extent of their efforts to a court who is listening to a plaintiff's every word and looking for a mistake, a misrepresentation, an omission, or a way to establish an agency arrangement not previously thought to exist, or a way to provide the basis for assigning liability to both the salesperson and the broker.

Personal Liability

In many states, the broker is personally liable for everything, regardless of any corporate entity which may exist. Damages from litigation, not to mention the attorney's fees, can run in the tens of thousands of dollars, ruining years of work and an otherwise promising and profitable career. It is time to learn from the policies and practices of the large professional companies in other fields of endeavor by creating a professional paper trail.

Clients and Customers as Plaintiffs

The Uniform Care and Feeding of Plaintiffs

Real estate professionals are, by nature, a helpful and trusting group of individuals that spend a small concentrated amount of time with strangers and start to treat them like lifelong friends. Treat all clients and customers as if they were going to be plaintiffs. Just because you have bought lunch or dinner for several days or shown someone houses and are now on a first name basis, do not let your guard down. Regard the other person as if he were an FBI agent or government tester. Your treatment of everyone should stand up to the closest scrutiny. Would you like to hear what you have just told someone played back on a tape recording in a court? If the answer is no, maybe you should not say it. This is not to say that you need to be anything other than a uniform, courteous, polite and detail-oriented professional.

Sources of Plaintiffs

Although through the subagency system you may be included in some litigation merely from being the listing broker and allowing subagency, as almost every broker today does, most of the plaintiffs that you will deal with will come from your own list of client, customer, and lender contacts. Look over the people you are willing to throw your career away for and think.

More often than not plaintiffs fall into two catagories: First, plaintiffs often turn out to be people that you thought were close friends. Ask yourself: Is this because they expected more than you normally deliver or because you used a standard for friends different from the one you use with your regular clients? Whom would you cancel an appointment with first, a new client or an old friend? Second, plaintiffs arise from those people who should not surprise you as you felt all along they were trouble. It is rare for a complaint to come from an average customer or client. When in doubt, treat someone like a stranger, and try not to treat strangers like friends.

Profile of a Plaintiff

Look at your customer, client, and lender lists for people with the following characteristics. Invariably I find they make great potential plaintiffs:

1. Someone who envies the material possessions of others.

2. Someone who feels that the world is not fair to them.

3. Someone who tells you about the poor conduct of another real estate professional, lawyer, doctor or lender. You may be next in line.

4. Someone who confides in you. Personally, I do not need to know secrets because I cannot tell them to anyone. They only contaminate my mind and thought process.

5. Someone in a position of apparent authority—a loan officer, an attorney, another broker—who suggests that some action or statement is either correct or incorrect in direct contradiction to what you know to be true.

6. Someone who wants to "get away" with something, wants to avoid paying a legally just obligation, or who thinks there is a way to "get around" the rules, especially loan qualification procedures and financial disclosure requirements.

Myths about Disclaimers

1. Disclaimers have to be stuffy and dry to be effective.

2. Disclaimers, if actually read by the addressee, will kill the deal. No one will buy this property if I have to tell them all that.

3. Oral disclaimers are just as good as written ones.

4. The buyers and sellers I deal with are my friends; I do not need a disclaimer for them.

5. Someone else said it, and, even if I know it is false, the fact that someone else made the statement is enough to get me off the hook.

6. Only attorneys can or should write appropriate and adequate disclaimers.

7. Even though the company policy prescribes the use of this form, I can just change a few words and it will do the same job.

8. Buyers do not need disclaimers.

9. I can always give the disclaimer after the showing, after the contract is signed or even at the closing. It will be just as effective.

10. No one really cares about or reads a disclaimer.

11. An adequate disclaimer will cover any mistake I might make, no matter how wrong I was.

12. Disclaimers are like indemnification agreements.

13. I do not need a disclaimer because our company has errors and omissions insurance.

14. Disclaimers are like an insurance policy; they always provide ample protection.

The Work Habit

Friend or Foe?

Are you your own best friend or worst enemy? The manner in which you regularly conduct your business is admissible evidence to demonstrate that there is a pattern of practice, whether it be good or bad, relevant to discrimination, price fixing, negligence, or competency. It is like having good manners. If you have them, they work when you do not think about them. A pattern of good conduct can show a court, judge and jury that you are a careful and consistent professional. Once that has been established, you can win one case using the procedures you always use day to day in the conduct of your business as demonstrated in other cases.

Pattern of Practice

On the other hand, the most frequently utilized tool of the opposition is to establish a pattern of practice that tends to discredit the witness. This is a killer, even if, in this instance, you actually did do and say the things that you claim. No protection system will work unless you establish a pattern of conduct, a reputation, a history of doing things correctly. Believe it or not, professionals who draft comprehensive cover letters are respected by their clients and customers and receive the coveted referral. The perception of such conduct is one of professionalism and attention to detail. This coveted reputation is better than "he is a real tough person." It becomes, "she is a real stickler and a professional. She will have all her paperwork in order. Suing her is a waste of time." No one wants to start, pay for, work on, or take a losing suit to court. Fifty percent of all lawyers lose. The difference is often in aligning oneself with a winning case.

The First Trial

The first place your case will be tried is in the office of the other lawyer. He will never admit defeat to you in front of his client. However, after you leave, you want him to say to his client. "Did you see how organized they were and the paperwork they had," or "I believe they are telling the truth. They were so professional." He will realize that you probably did send the documents you said you sent and did explain to his client the areas that you said you explained and that there is a good possibility that his client is lying. No civil attorney, except possibly the government, wants a client he knows, or fears, is lying; it can rub off on the attorney who frequently appears in the same court. The retainer demanded by opposing council after such a meeting, formerly $1,000, is now $3,000.

Company Protection Policies

Office Manual

Establishing a manual containing specific procedures to be followed in each transaction, a routine and formal mechanical treatment of all the company's clients and customers is the best first line of defense. A manual allows the agents to concentrate on selling real estate rather than on worrying about the need for and the exact wording of disclaimers, informational and other letters, and contract clauses. It is all there when you need it. All well-drafted manuals should be capable of becoming reading material for even the most discriminating individuals, such as regulators, opposing counsel, clients, customers and the commission.

Standard Forms

Standard forms are the only answer. Attorneys have used them for years and are consistently developing new ones. This is not because they are lazy or stupid. Quite the reverse, they realize that the thought process that went into the last problem can be utilized on the next similar problem and duplicated without having to rethink and plan for the problems previously presented and solved.

Brochure

One or more company brochures which include a list of the services offered, the fees charged, if appropriate, and a series of checklists for the client, customer, agent, and the company is quite valuable. It is a good way to explain to everyone in a uniform and consistent manner what services are and are not available, what is expected of each party to a proposed transaction, and the amount to be charged for each respective service. This is especially useful in discouraging unwanted property management, listed as a separate item with its own cost analysis. A set of company policy statements or brochures, well-drafted and with good content and type styles can be a great protection device, insure uniformity of information given out, and serve notice of established company policies. The use of comprehensive checklists for all stages of any transaction removes the sense of uncertainty as to what tasks need to be completed. Having these expectations in writing greatly reduces the level of stress experienced by both the salesperson in the field and the broker. Then it is no longer necessary to rely on memory for all the required steps in a transaction.

Standard Practices

Standardization, company wide, is a must. You accomplish it by creating a complete program that includes the use of only those forms and clauses that have been approved by the state, if applicable, and by the company. The use of a series of approved cover letters for each stage of a transaction should be coupled with a schedule for their step-by-step distribution.

When a transaction does not fit the standard, it must receive broker attention. Discouraging the on-the-spot modification of standard forms and procedures for the unusual transaction is imperative. It is these transactions that have the highest degree of risk. This way the broker knows that each client and customer is getting the standard information, the required disclosures, and the same set of instructions. In addition, the agent does not have to allow herself to be pressured into making a decision that might not be in anyone's best interests. It removes the need to improvise and allows everyone to concentrate on the listing, sale, and closing of real estate transactions that will not result in future problems. How to gain that kind of surefootedness is what this book is about.

Tips for Early Disaster Recognition

1. Be alert. Watch for the unusual in the usual.

2. Above all be consistent. Treat everyone and every transaction in the same manner. No special deals.

3. If it seems too good to be true it probably is. When things do not seem correct or you do not feel comfortable, talk with your broker or your attorney immediately. Things have a way of moving quickly when they are going the wrong way.

4. Have a personal attorney whom you respect, who is above reproach, and whom you can talk to when you feel the need.

5. As soon as the deal starts to look funny, get away from it and make your departure known. If you are leaving a formal meeting, be sure that your departure is noted in the minutes. In other circumstances remember those people who in turn will remember the timing of your departure.

6. Make your notes as contemporaneously as possible and retain them. Note what occurs in each transaction and at all meetings. Write letters to your broker, or as a broker, to your salespersons. Document your position

and policy in writing, not just by oral conferences. Should you elect to resign, a letter of resignation stating the reasons for your actions is important.

7. If the communication is with a client or a customer, a witness who is not a relative or associate is invaluable.

8. Tape recordings are a very useful tool. I am sorry to have to say this, but the tape recorder keeps honest people's memories in sync. It has literally saved the reputation and fortune of many of my clients.

9. Be true to yourself. You know when things are wrong. You will remember what happened and worry about the potential repercussions long after the money has been spent.

The Referral

You will live or die by your referrals. Be sure that whoever you recommend meets your standards. There is never a need to refer a person to anyone if the association will not be to your direct benefit. If the customer is pleased with your referral, you will get a little emotional pat on the back some of the time and maybe a thank you. If there is any problem, the customer will try to hold you responsible, and you will suffer the financial and emotional consequences of the customer's displeasure.

Tips, Tricks, and Traps

Certified Mail vs. Regular Mail

If it is important enough to send by certified or registered mail, you should *also* send it by regular mail. There is a lattice of different regulations for each state; some matters require one form of mail, some allow for the other. In addition, there are a lot of cases that indicate that simply sending a letter by certified or registered mail is not sufficient to constitute delivery or notice, especially if the addressee does not claim the letter. A better procedure is to send two identical copies of the letter, one certified or registered, and the other regular mail. Indicate if you wish, on the original, prior to photocopying, "Original Sent Certified Mail" and "Copy Sent Regular Mail." If this is your established practice when you send certified or registered mail, it will be seen as proof that, in fact, that is what you did for the matter in question.

Confirmation

A good alternative to a letter that requires an affirmative act—such as the signature of the reader, which is often difficult to obtain—is the confirming letter. The confirming letter shifts the burden of action to the reader. This is a very convenient method for confirming the content and timeliness of an oral statement. In addition, it firmly places the responsibility to act on the reader if the content does not match his or her understanding of what was said. Many people who will not take the step of signing the disclosure statement, will also not take the time and effort to deny the facts as outlined in a confirming letter: "This is to confirm our discussion of last Tuesday wherein I indicated..." This practice not only gives you a favorable legal standing but also provides good service. It helps keep the good deals good and brings the bad, time-wasting or dangerous ones to the forefront.

Copies

An indication on the letter of who is to receive copies can be a good record of where copies of the letter were actually sent. You can even include the addresses to which a copy was sent if you wish. This puts the reader on notice that you are letting others know of the activities described in the letter. This is a good method of advising everyone of action being taken. It can discourage people from contesting the fact that they received the mailing and the truth of its contents. It is also a courtesy since the letter is no longer private. Think of the time-saving advantages of telling everyone exactly the same information at the same time. Make a habit of including this common notation at the bottom of your letters. Example:

cc: Oliver E. Frascona, Esq.
4750 Table Mesa Drive
Boulder, CO 80303
Hon. William Armstrong, U.S. Senator

A note about including senators and congressmen on your copy list: Most of elected officials take their mail seriously. Only include them when you actually send a copy to such an individual and then only when the copy has a specific purpose. Sending miscellaneous mail to such offices is a lot like crying wolf.

Copies—Blind

There are occasions when you do not want to indicate who received a copy. In such instances you would omit the copy information, but always remember to note on your copy the people who actually received a copy.

Dates

No matter what you write it on, always date all correspondence. It is a good habit to date and initial, or make a mark known only to you, in the lower left or right hand corner of everything you draft, approve or review.

Formality

Everyone wants to be treated like the corporate executive. People perceive that such individuals always get formal letters. More important, the court will place a greater significance on a formal letter than on an informal one, especially if disclosure is the issue. Compliment the reader. Treat him like an ambassador. Formal letters can read in an easy manner. They need not be stiff.

Frequency

When in doubt, write a letter. It is hard to imagine sending too many letters. Contact is the first step to contentment, and it establishes care and concern. Most people just want to know what is going on so that they can adjust their plans accordingly. Communication is almost always the key. Lack of communication is one of the three most often listed causes of litigation.

Letterhead

Always write all your letters on letterhead if possible, and always keep a copy for your file. Like a business card, letterhead exudes credibility and makes a statement about you.

Margins and Spacing

These little things accomplish a lot. Ragged right margins are more friendly and less formal. They tend to get more attention and are read more frequently. In addition, they give a personal touch to a standard letter.

Right-justified margins are more standoffish and receive less scrutiny. Right-justified margins are useful to indicate that your office is modern, organized, has a word processor or other automated document-preparation capability, and a standard procedure for completing your professional tasks.

That they also tend to attract less scrutiny may or may not be beneficial, depending on your message.

Mechanics

No one will ever know what you know, nor will they be able to open your head and look inside. Most of us will be judged by our paperwork and personality. There is never an excuse for poor grammar or punctuation. They leave the reader with a sense that the author is not a professional.

Whiteout is not only an invitation to modification, but it is personally unacceptable for my work. I always enjoy whiteout on colored paper. If someone cannot prepare a crisp, clean letter, how will they do with my contract documents and the important things such as deeds, notes, and the like?

Memorandum of Previous Oral Conversation

When the cow is not only out of the barn but is hamburger, and you need to cover the tracks, this is a very useful tool utilized by many attorneys. You start your communication with the words, "This is a memorandum of our previous oral conversation of Friday, June 28th, 1910," and follow with the body of what you indicated in that previous oral conversation. This serves to document your disclosure, not as of the date of the memorandum, but as of the date the conversation took place. This is not always a fail-safe system because the other party may refuse to sign, may deny the fact of the previous conversation and even controvert it, which could put you in a more difficult position than had you not tried this tactic. Use it only when the outcome is known.

Personal Touch

If you utilize a word processor, try to make the variables in a letter more than just the name and address of the reader. Include little facts about the transaction or the property to make the form letter as personal to the reader as possible. Do not change the standard boiler plate language established by your office. It is there for your protection, as well as for the protection of the firm and the broker.

Re:

This designator on the letter means "regarding" or "in regards to" and indicates what it is you are talking about. A general reference, or no reference at all, attracts less attention to the particular matter than a specific reference. Specific references are useful for many letters where you want to be sure the reader's attention is focused on the issue. Help your readers know what the main subject is right away—and establish the reference for rapid identification when you see the letter later on—by leading off your letters with a specific "Re:" line just above the salutation. If you want the letter to receive less attention, eliminate the "Re:" entirely or make it vague and uninviting.

Structure

Start every communication, especially a letter, with something pleasant that compliments the reader or makes him feel at ease. Put your reader in the right frame of mind for the content of the letter.

The body of the letter should be polite and tactful but always explicit, especially when it is a disclaimer that you are conveying. Mix several ideas in a single letter to equalize the content between disclaimer and information. A long letter is a good place to include a lot of serious disclaimers you do not want someone to dwell upon, as it will probably never get the reader's full attention and yet will cover the notification process. Several separate letters serve to keep the reader informed but each will receive closer scrutiny. This is a good way to convey good news or routine information. When you want to be sure they read it, keep it short.

The closing should always be polite and offer your assistance: "If there is anything I can do to assist you, please do not hesitate to let me know." "Thank you for your cooperation and assistance in this matter." "We are happy to be your agents." "It is always a pleasure to have you as a client." Even if the content of the letter is difficult, always make the closing pleasant.

Typed vs. Handwritten

A typed letter or statement is always the better selection. Typed material is easier to read. However, a handwritten letter is far better than none at all.

Drafting Ideas

Abbreviations

If at all possible, do not abbreviate anything. Spell it out. I always wonder who David is in the statement "David and Joan Farus." David who? Farus? It could be David Copperfield. The absence of abbreviations is a sign of professionalism, reduces the need to make assumptions, and avoids misunderstandings.

Checks and Endorsements

When a check is made payable to you and you are about to endorse it, especially if the endorsement is to constitute a release, add these words: "Modification or alteration of this restrictive endorsement makes this check void."

Drafts

Try hard never to let your first draft be the final draft. Doing the first draft in pencil will force you to rewrite the letter or the contract at least once. You will always do a better job the second time. Another useful tool is a rubber stamp marked "DRAFT for DISCUSSION PURPOSES ONLY."

The enemy is misunderstanding. Clear documents go a long way to eliminate rather than foster misunderstanding. Try it for a while and see if your second or third drafts create a better final product.

Days and Dates

The rules vary from state to state; however, generally, unless specified otherwise, references to dates are to calendar days. If you want to avoid any possible misunderstandings, specify "calendar" or "business" days.

Exhibits

The proper wording is "The attached Exhibit A-Legal Description, consisting of ___ pages, is incorporated herein and hereby made a part of this document by this reference." Even if you do not use all of that, try to give each exhibit a title as well as a letter. There can be a lot of legal descriptions marked "Exhibit A" when a stack of documents is dropped. Another useful trick is to number each client or transaction and place that number on all documents that affect the transaction. If in doubt you can use the street address.

Originals

Any document that has an original signature is an original document. There is no substitute for an original. Let the other people have copies. If everyone wants an original, make duplicate originals, several identical copies all with original signatures. If there are a lot of changes to a document, other than a cover letter, make the changes, photocopy the altered original, and sign the photocopies as originals. You must retain a copy of every letter sent and every signed document that passes through your hands. The good record keepers are hard to discredit. Be one of them.

Realtor®

This is a registered mark belonging to the National Association of Realtors® (NAR) which may be used by its members in the fashion designated by NAR. It should always be followed by the ® symbol. Realtors® should avoid its use generically in speech , in contracts, in the proper name of their company, or as a synonym for a person who is a real estate licensee, even if such licensee is a member of NAR. If you have additional questions or are concerned about the proper use of the mark, an extensive guide dealing with the use of the Realtor® mark is available from NAR.

Receipts

A fast and efficient system to insure that you can describe the document received by the recipient is to have a self-inking rubber stamp made that looks something like the example below. Simply make a copy of the document, stamp it, and get the signature of the recipient. It's a fast, accurate, and efficient system that does not require a lot of thought. It is also convenient when you are trusting someone else who might not be aware of the importance of or the description of the particular document or not know what to write on a receipt. Red, with large letters, seems to be the most useful.

The undersigned hereby receipts for the original of this document consisting of _____ pages, on the date indicated.

_____   _____
Recipient   Date

Notaries and Witnesses

I am convinced that if I am merely present during a transaction, no matter how much I disavow my role, someone will hold me responsible for something. As a result I never allow anyone to sign whose identity I have not verified and who does not sign in my presence. The number of forged notary signatures, a form of state-approved witness with a seal, would destroy your faith in people.

Case in Point

A notary testified, under oath, that she saw Nancy sign a document she had notarized. There was no doubt in her mind that Nancy and Fred had appeared before her personally and were the signatories. She could even pick out Nancy now from the present group, standing next to Fred. Imagine her surprise when she was informed that the lady standing next to Fred was really named Roberta, his girl friend, and not Nancy, Fred's wife.

The story got even better when it was learned that the individual who had signed Nancy's name was a man, not Roberta, not Nancy, and not present. Once you have been with a stranger for a few days, you too might be tempted to notarize her signature. Require the proper identification with every signature.

Term Definition

A nice way to define a term for later use is to enclose it in parentheses with quotation marks after the first use of the word. The real property ("Property"). Thereafter, you can simply refer to it as the Property. This helps your letter be precise without being wordy and gives it that professional appearance.

Chapter Two

Obtaining the Listing

The Listing Presentation

The broker, being responsible for the entire world and, very often, for several well-meaning salespersons, is concerned that the new potential seller understand several principles at the start of what could be a lasting relationship. In most states, the listing is the property of the broker, and the broker is personally liable not only for his own actions and inaction but also for that of the salespersons whose licenses hang under the broker's license.

To that end, the broker wants to make sure that the potential client understands several legal principles and the procedures followed by the broker's firm. Most important, the broker desires to limit the apparent authority of the salesperson in the client's eye by defining the extent of such authority early in the relationship. A nice cover letter after the first contact by the agent can accomplish these objectives. If you have a firm brochure or printed statement that can accompany this letter, the letter should include a specific reference to the brochure, the pertinent disclaimer or the firm policy statement.

Not all of the following items need to be addressed in the first letter, but they will serve as a checklist of items that need to be addressed sooner or later. Some are mentioned in different letters, since putting them all in the first letter could be overwhelming. Different sellers may require more or fewer of these items in the first letter. As these items are discussed, the seller will start to get a feeling about the agent, the broker, the firm, and the complexities of modern real estate. This can be a very good marketing tool because the seller begins to realize that this is an area where a professional is a necessity and that you are the professional to employ.

How many of us get a personal letter from the broker talking about our house? This indicates a level of interest that impresses a potential client.

Agency and Apparent Authority

Establish early the fact that you, as the broker, exist, that you are party to the transaction, that you and you alone bind the firm, and that you are available for problem-solving and consultation. Also establish early the extent of the agency relationship which is being created and reinforce it often. Itemize exactly what the broker and salesperson will do for the client, what they will not do, and what is expected of the client. Limit or eliminate the apparent authority of the salesperson to bind the broker or the firm. This can be an advantage to the broker, firm, and salesperson because the seller now knows the limit of the salesperson's authority to make certain decisions and that the salesperson cannot bind the broker in most matters.

The actions or inactions of the salesperson or the broker may serve to override the information and disclaimers given at any point in time, and, therefore, the constant reference to the extent of authority or lack thereof is important. You cannot say it once, act in direct contradiction to the written statements, and hope to be protected. Conduct speaks louder than promises and will be the ultimate determining factor.

Anti-Trust and Commissions

Deal with any anti-trust commission and cooperative split problems if you feel they might be present. Clearly establish the commission policies of the firm. This will make the salesperson's job of presenting or negotiating the commission much easier and will establish that the broker has the right to split the total commission if the broker so desires. It is important for the broker to indicate early on that the broker retains the exclusive right to determine if there will be a split, the amount of such a split, and the terms upon which the broker will pay the cooperating broker.

Too frequently, after the broker has become obligated to a particular cooperating broker, the seller determines that the seller should enter into the decision-making process. If you wish, set forth here the rules, if any, for such splits. I would discourage this, except in the instances of the modifications that may occur when the buyer uses the services of a buyer's broker at the buyer's expense and therefore tries to modify the price offered to the seller and the commission that the broker will be entitled to from the seller.

Brochure

If you do not have a standard brochure or firm position statement, you might consider drafting one along the lines of the model letters in this book. A brochure is a good medium for standardizing the information that is presented to the public before you have the opportunity to correct or clarify it with a cover letter to any one prospect.

Condition of the Property

The seller, not the broker, is going to represent the condition of the property. Most firms have an addendum to the listing contract that allows the seller to designate the current condition of the property. Adding to this a recitation of one's reliance on the seller's representations may provide an incentive to be more specific and accurate and provide the broker with additional protection. The trend is to hold the broker responsible for defects he could have discovered, even though he did not actually discover them.

Earnest Money

He who holds the earnest money will surely be the center of attention when a dispute arises. Almost without exception, there is nothing you can or should do to distribute the money without a written statement from both parties. You cannot make a determination on the merits of each party's application for the funds nor determine if a default has occurred. That inability to act will put you in an awkward position. Now is the time to explain to the seller the laws relating to earnest money. Point out the contract wording in the sales contract that deals with earnest money. Explain your limits early.

Control of the earnest money may or may not pose a problem. Generally, it is a contract term and therefore the parties can designate who will retain the earnest money. As the seller's agent, you want control of the money or the direction to designate on your seller's behalf who shall have control. Except for the good relationship you will have with your bank as the result of the funds sitting in your account, there is little benefit in holding earnest money. I would advise you to try to let someone else hold earnest money. Title companies are always willing to accept this type of position. In any event, the preferred repository designated by the seller and the minimum amount that the seller requires with any offer need to be discussed.

Fair Housing

Clear the air and establish the rules early with regard to The Fair Housing Law. People, especially testers, appreciate frankness and will respect you for your knowledge of the law. You are protecting the seller against potential problems as well as yourself. If there is going to be a problem here, it is better to know it very early.

Financing

Start the seller thinking about the ever-increasing list of alternatives. Present to the seller the basic description of certain types of financing that are available and that may be suggested by potential buyers. Describe the potential impact of the general forms of financing on the seller and how each of the alternatives likely to arise in this transaction will affect the salability of the property. Documenting the discussion of financing is becoming very important as financing alternatives vary in complexity and in the effect they may have on sellers in varying situations.

Hazardous Materials

With the advent of concern about radon gas, chemical spills, buried waste materials and the like, it is often impossible for the broker to know what may be lurking below the surface. The only adequate form of protection is to have experts test the premises—much as is done in many parts of the country for termites—and make the report available to potential purchasers before they contract for the property. The alternative is to wait to see if the buyer will require any tests as a condition precedent to closing. Then, however, a lot of time has passed before you know if you have a deal.

More and more relocation companies are refusing to purchase properties that have not had a radon test. Many times, in order to take advantage of the company buy-out program when the buyer later sells, he will require a radon gas test because the existence of a satisfactory inspection prior to his acquiring ownership will be a requirement for later buy-out. The proper tests need to be encouraged and performed by recognized experts as soon as possible after the listing is signed. Indicating this to the seller before or immediately after obtaining the listing will add to your credibility as an expert, support the correct perception that marketing a home is complex, and protect you from later—sometimes years later—having to explain why you did not test the property. Such tests are generally a seller's expense; therefore, extracting the money to pay for the test or having the seller agree to pay the tester directly is important.

Inspections, Engineers and Home Warranties

The use of inspectors to limit the broker's and salesperson's liability for all sorts of potential problems, although not mandatory, is certainly a recommended practice. Acquainting the seller early on with the idea that various other professionals will be required to complete the transaction serves to indicate areas that are not within the purview of the agency relationship and not among the list of tasks that the real estate firm provides. The cost, the availability of home warranty services, and the extent of their coverage need to be explained at the outset of the relationship.

Liability—Premises and Open Houses

Explain the limits of the company's liability and the need to inventory property of unusual value. Give a review of the people who will seek access to the property and the measures that are in place to restrict, limit, or supervise such access. The fact that the broker will not be responsible for anything except gross negligence must be presented.

Discuss the office "Open House" policy and its beneficial use as a marketing tool. Acknowledge the quiet concern people have about having other people in their home. Strangers and neighbors who have not before had access to the home will now potentially have access and possibly become aware of personal items. Present the benefits, liabilities, and potential problems and let the client decide. Be clear that the client can always reserve the decision for a later time.

Liability—Lock Boxes

Present the lock box system used by your office and the possible security problems that exist with any listing that utilizes the lock box system. People will appreciate your care for their possessions. Although it may be a system with substantial problems, such as a system with one key for all boxes or one that uses boxes easily opened or destroyed by unauthorized people, it may be a marketing necessity. The decision to use a lock box must be clearly the seller's. If you have a superior system in operation for your company, this would be a good time to point out its comparative advantages. Still, however, explain the limits of the company's liability.

Mortgage Insurance Premiums

With the advent of prepaid FHA mortgage insurance, the mortgage insurance which may be a part of a transaction has increased significantly. Whether it should be prorated or included as a part of the purchase price—especially in a transaction that calls for an assumption of an existing policy—can mean a substantial amount of money for the seller to receive and for the buyer to part with. Adequately explaining the alternatives and effects of each selection, as well as the method of proration, is important. As the amount of the insurance premium comes closer and closer to the total commission, your portion of the commission becomes an obvious source of funds for adjustment in the event of a dispute.

Multiple Listing Service

Explain the broker's membership in, access to, the operation of, and the confidential nature of information contained in the Multiple Listing Service. Also indicate that, although the information in the MLS is not to be totally relied upon because it is there only for member brokers' use and not for the general public, it is your desire that the listing be accurate to the last detail. Encourage the seller's review of the MLS information sheet, which is attached to some states' listing contracts, in order to establish that it accurately presents the facts about the property.

Pricing

The price that you will allow the seller to ask and still accept the listing is a very touchy area. If you establish the price, you may be liable for its determination. You may also lead the seller to believe that you are an appraiser, and that may set you up for future liability if the market proves you wrong. Therefore, I discourage the broker or the salesperson from attempting to establish the price.

Some firms have a limit on the amount of what they feel is "blue sky," or overpricing. They are unwilling to work on listings that are priced so high that the property will probably not sell within the listing period and therefore not be worth the effort and expense. Accepting an overpriced listing and not working on it or disparaging it to fellow real estate agents is asking for trouble. Try to capture the listing at a reasonable price, established by the seller, and boost the professional image of the salesperson and firm. This can be accomplished professionally by providing the seller with the information that you have available about comparable sales and current listings and letting the seller suggest the listing price. At that time you can determine if in fact it is worth your effort.

Soils Condition

Much as with the tests for hazardous materials, a soils test or report may alleviate a lot of problems later on. A report from a soils engineer is not too expensive and should be encouraged. If any damage is evident, an inspection and a report indicating what action is recommended should be strongly encouraged. It too will become a condition later on and possibly result in lost marketing time during a prime season. It goes without saying that the report must be given to all prospective purchasers before they are under contract.

Structural Integrity vs. Mechanical Integrity

Engineers are the experts with regard to the structural integrity of the dwelling. Generally, they do not pass on the physical or operating condition of the various mechanical devices located on the property. Mechanical inspections and the subsequent insurance are available from a variety of competitors. The buyer and seller often operate under the misconception, convenient or innocent, that the mechanical inspection also covers the structure. Clear recommendations indicating the talents and scope of the different classes of inspectors and their resultant coverages will limit the valid future claims of a buyer looking for either a way out of the transaction or someone to help with the monthly payments.

Subagency Alternatives and Potential Dual Agency

Describe the various alternative types of potential subagents or buyers' brokers, their relationship to the seller, the salesperson, and the broker. Review compensation of the various forms of other agents. Many people are in the dark about this system of agents and brokers working together. Help them understand. Their new knowledge will confirm their confidence in you and also in the extent of the professional network that is available to assist in the sale of their property.

This may even serve as a start on the protection system in the case of a seller who turns into a buyer. I know the first thing we all do when a seller, whose listing we have or have had, asks to see other real estate is to tell the seller that we are no longer his agent and are now acting as the subagent for all the other sellers out there. Right? Giving a full and proper rendition of the subagency alternatives when the property is listed may serve to limit these future problems. But then there is no real cause for concern, after all the old seller is now a friend, and we all know that friends are "safe" and do not need the normal disclosures that mere customers and clients would receive.

If your firm allows both buyer representation and seller representation, agents to purchase properties listed with the firm, or other transactions that provide potential conflicts of interest, this is the time to explain in specific detail exactly what the relationship will be in such an event. If you are looking for trouble, dual agency is the ultimate black hole.

Listing Concerns

DENVER CANADIAN
REALTY, INC.
420 Ponderosa Drive   Boulder, CO 80303
(303) 494-6661

Mr. and Mrs. Gary S. Joiner
4750 Table Mesa Drive
Boulder, CO 80303

    Re: 75 McCoy Drive, Windhaven

Dear Mr. and Mrs. Joiner:

Please let me introduce myself. I am the licensed broker for Denver Canadian Realty, Inc. I have just spoken with Jim Smittkamp who has been describing your home in detail to me. I must say he is very excited and feels that he can market it successfully on the terms and conditions you have established as the agent for this office, if we are selected to be your listing agents.

When you list with this company, through Jim, you also obtain the cooperative efforts of the rest of our professionally trained agents and our entire office staff of support personnel. I have included a brochure describing the services that we as a team provide to our clients. If you have time, please look it over because it describes all of the various services that we provide, the areas that you are responsible for, the areas that we both have no control over, some valuable information about the complexities involved in modern real estate, and why I am proud to be the responsible broker for this office.

The following are a few little items that I like to discuss with each potential new client. Please read each one carefully and feel free to call me if you wish to discuss any item in more detail. I am happy to talk about real estate and your listing at any time. My home number is 494-4664.

Fair Housing

This firm is proud to display the Housing and Urban Development (HUD) Equal Housing Opportunity Poster, "We do business in accordance with the Federal Fair Housing Law," and we take the Civil Rights Act of 1968 and the Housing and Community Development Act of 1974 very seriously. It is illegal to discriminate against any person because of race, color, religion, sex, national origin or age. We are happy to say that all of the agents in our office have signed the Affirmative Marketing Agreement previously requested of all real estate agents by HUD.

As real estate professionals, we are pledged to providing equal access for every potential purchaser to all locations and types of housing that are available in this area as may be selected by the customers who inquire about housing. I know you are happy to know that we, as your agents, will show your home to anyone regardless of their race, creed, color, national origin, religious preference, heritage, age, sex, etc. We make sure that every potential customer knows that your house is available and is made aware of the features that it offers. This helps protect you as a seller since you too must follow the Federal Fair Housing Law.

Anti-Trust

One item you see in the proposed listing contract is the commission that our office charges for a listing such as yours. Jim indicated that you felt everyone "charged the same fee." Whether that is the case or not is unknown to me and not really relevant to this firm which is cost-service conscious. We decide what our services are worth based on many things: the quality of service we provide, the number of listings that we feel we can properly and successfully market in a given period, the time estimated for the sale of various listings, the price ranges of listings that we hope to market, and the overall cost of doing business in today's market. If other firms price their services at a similar or equal rate, that comes from their own analysis and is solely their concern. We feel that the level of professionalism and the degree of success that we attain for our clients justifies our commission rate. I think that after you have had the opportunity to experience our services, you will agree. The amount of commission we charge is one of the items that I alone am responsible for and I would be glad to discuss it at length with you if you so desire.

Our firm offers to potential subagents a portion of the total commission that we receive in order to encourage them to show and sell your home. The amount of such compensation and the terms upon which we will pay the same to another real estate agent are totally within our discretion and are based upon various factors. There is no standard commission split or "co-op" rate in this area. The Local Area Board of Realtors® does not set or control any commission rates nor the amount or percentage to be paid to subagents.

Realtor®

We are proud to be members of the National Association of Realtors® through our affiliation with the Local Area Board of Realtors®. This means that we adhere to the Code of Ethics and participate in the various educational opportunities that are available to members of the board. If you have any questions about what it means to be a Realtor®, please give me a call. Not every person licensed by this state to sell real estate is a Realtor®.

Multiple Listing Service

This firm is a member of the Mulitple Listing Service (MLS), and, therefore, we can place your listing in the Multiple Listing Book for numerous other agents to review. Before we do this, we will submit the information as it will appear in the MLS so that you can review it and insure that it is accurate. It's an extra step; but no one knows your home better than you do, and we want to be sure that everything we publish will detail your home's available options and features as accurately as we both can make them. Although the MLS includes a statement indicating that it is for the exclusive use of member brokers and that the information contained therein is not to be strictly relied upon, we want our listings to be accurate.

Buyer Brokerage and Sellers' Subagents

Other firms may become exposed to your home as the result of our advertising in various publications, or through marketing meetings and breakfasts, the Multiple Listing Service, and the other efforts of Jim Smittkamp and the other agents of this firm. These firms, acting through their agents, have a choice as to whether they are going to act as agents for their customers, which would make them buyers' brokers, or as our agents, meaning your subagents, when they contact us to show and sell your home. Subagents work through their firm but represent you as subagents of the seller. Therefore, they owe their loyalty to both of us. Buyers' brokers are agents for the purchaser and do not represent either of us. This firm feels that we should encourage anyone who is interested in your home to purchase it. Therefore, we encourage the cooperation of both subagents and buyers' brokers. We reserve the right, however, to pay either type of agent, in accordance to that agent's services, that portion of the total commission which we feel is appropriate, regardless of the agency relationship of the cooperating agent. You are cautioned against making any statements to other brokers or salespersons as it is often hard to determine where their allegiances lie. Likewise, we treat all inquiries as though they came from buyers' brokers to insure that your confidences are maintained.

Earnest Money

The policy in this state is that any entity selected by the parties can be the holder of the earnest money deposit. It is the policy of this firm that we, as the listing brokerage company, in lieu of direction from you to the contrary, will be the depository of the funds. These funds are actually placed in a separate bank account, segregated from all other accounts. Unless everyone agrees to the contrary, the earnest money is not placed in an interest-bearing account. The need to have the interest accrue to a specific social security number or federal ID number makes the routine setup and payout from such an account a nightmare. If, however, the amount is large or the term of its retention long in duration, an interest-bearing account is an alternative we are happy to consider.

Over the years this company has adopted a policy of encouraging the parties to select an escrow agent to accept earnest money deposits, other than Denver Canadian Realty, Inc. This independent escrow agent will accept, retain, and disburse any funds that are associated with your real estate transactions. This procedure ensures an impartial stakeholder, reduces bookkeeping, and removes us from any dispute that may arise with regard to the disposition of any such funds in the future. By law, we are not authorized to make any determination with regard to the entitlement of anyone to any portion of the earnest money in the event of a dispute.

Dual Agency

The possibility exists that one of our agents will, in the course of representing another seller, that is, another client of this firm, be placed in a position similar to that of a buyer's broker. This most often occurs when another seller determines that she is interested in your home. In that instance, absent written instructions from you to the contrary, and in an effort to sell your home, we cannot be held to our fiduciary duties. We simply are not responsible for any loss that may be sustained as a result of such a situation. The possibility exists that confidential information concerning your property or personal financial condition, disclosed to a member of this firm in confidence, will become available to the other client of this firm. For this reason I encourage you to deal directly with Jim and me for the review of any confidential information you wish to impart to us.

Agent Purchasing for His Own Account

As a general rule, this firm does not allow agents to purchase any property that we have listed. Exceptions are made in unusual situations. First, the same rules that are indicated above for Dual Agency apply. This firm is simply not responsible for any loss that you may sustain as the result of the buyer having access to confidential information. In addition, I present all such contracts personally, and each contract contains an indication that the agent is purchasing the property for his own account with the intention of making a profit. In all such situations, we encourage agents to submit only full-price offers. Should you be inclined to provide financing for such a buyer, which we discourage, we are not responsible in any way in the event that the buyer does not make the payments or adhere to any other aspect of the contract, the closing, or the financing documentation. We realize that we are missing a unique opportunity to be involved in litigation, but nevertheless wish to try to limit from the outset what is by definition a bad situation.

We look forward to having your home in our inventory of available homes. It is always a pleasure to have a well-kept and well-maintained home such as yours in our inventory of available listings.

Most Sincerely,
Denver Canadian Realty, Inc.

Rima E. Tormay

by: Rima E. Tormay, Broker

DENVER CANADIAN
REALTY, INC.
420 Ponderosa Drive   Boulder, CO 80303
(303) 494-6661

Mr. Gary S. Joiner
Mrs. Karen A. Joiner
4750 Table Mesa Drive
Boulder, CO 80303

  Re: 75 McCoy Drive, Windhaven

Dear Gary and Karen:

  When I explain the new FHA mortgage insurance treatment to my customers, I always feel it would be nice to have a little explanation in written form to review since it has become a significant amount of money and the alternatives are not always clear to brokers, lawyers, closing agents, let alone sellers and buyers. This is a little overview for you to keep handy throughout your listing with me. If you want to discuss it at any time just let me know and I will try to explain it further.

  The general rule for items that have been prepaid by the seller is that the buyer purchases the unused portion of such expenses since the buyer will enjoy the benefits of the unused portion of the contract. Insurance is a typical example. The buyer either buys the balance of the seller's fire insurance policy, because the buyer will be covered for the remainder of the term, or the buyer obtains his own insurance and the seller is allowed to cancel his policy and receive a refund from the insurance company.

  FHA mortgage insurance, absent an agreement to the contrary, should be treated in the same manner. The problem that occurs with FHA mortgage insurance is two-fold. First, unlike most expenses, this is not an annual policy; it is a thirty-year policy fully paid in advance. The proration, that is, the division between the buyer and the seller of the unused portion of the prepaid premium, would substantially increase the amount of money that a buyer would need, and the amount that the seller would receive, upon the closing of the transaction.

  Second, the prepaid premium is not easily prorated. The computation tables that are available from the Department of Housing and Urban Development essentially load more of the premium into the first seven or eight years of the life of the policy. This means that as the policy goes through the first few years, more than 1/30th of the premium per year is considered as earned, and therefore not available in the event of a cancellation with each passing year. Essentially the proration is calculated as if the buyer, who would be the owner of the mortgage insurance policy, cashed it in for a refund on the date of closing. The amount the buyer would receive is the amount that would be allocated to the seller at the closing.

As I have indicated previously, in the event there is an offer that entails the assumption of your FHA loan, it is often not possible for the buyer to also bear the burden of the proration. Therefore, the buyer may ask that the prepaid insurance not be prorated. Not an equitable proposition. I shall continue to indicate that the FHA insurance must be prorated in addition to the listed price of your home. Much like our discussion of assumptions, this presents a decision that ultimately must be made by you when you receive an offer to purchase.

Thank you for letting me take the time to review this complex little area. Feel free to call if you want to talk it over some more.

Sincerely,
Denver Canadian Realty, Inc.

Jim Smittkamp

by: Jim Smittkamp, Sales Agent

cc: Lee D. Weinstein, Broker

DENVER CANADIAN
REALTY, INC.
420 Ponderosa Drive   Boulder, CO 80303
(303) 494-6661

Mr. Gary S. Joiner
Mrs. Karen A. Joiner
4750 Table Mesa Drive
Boulder, CO 80303

     Re: 75 McCoy Drive, Windhaven

Dear Gary and Karen:

    Jim and I and all the members of this firm are happy and proud to have been selected to market your home. Jim has been an agent with this company for 38 years and has assisted many people in both marketing their existing property and in selecting new real estate. As I am sure he indicated, all contractual obligations of Denver Canadian Realty Inc., to be effective under the law, must be formally approved by me as the licensed broker. This allows agents to concentrate on the marketing of your home, leaving the obligations of this firm to the broker.

    [Jim, although a licensed broker, and therefore qualified by the state to open his own office if he so desires, is acting in a broker-salesman capacity under my license for this company to assist you in the sale of your home.]

    I am happy to inform you that I, as the broker of Denver Canadian Realty Inc., have just accepted and countersigned your proposed Listing Agreement, including the Seller's Property Disclosure Addendum, as submitted by Jim Smittkamp. A copy of the fully executed Listing Agreement is enclosed for your records. Welcome to our list of clients.

    Jim has been describing your beautiful home, including your extensive well-cared-for garden, in detail to everyone in the office. I look forward to seeing your home personally on our office tour.

    Please feel free to contact me at any time should you wish to discuss any aspect of your real estate needs or your relationship with this company.

              Most sincerely,
              Denver Canadian Realty, Inc.

              Evelyn M. Ruka

              by: Evelyn M. Ruka, Broker

Mr. Gary S. Joiner
Mrs. Karen A. Joiner
4750 Table Mesa Drive
Boulder, CO 80303

    Re: 75 McCoy Drive, Windhaven

Dear Mr. and Mrs. Joiner:

The acquisition of a home is the largest purchase the average person will attempt in his lifetime. Real estate is becoming more complex and less liquid in this soft economy. Most people nowadays are convinced that the cautious buyer will make inquiry into the structural condition and mechanical condition of all prospective properties. To avoid making what might be interpreted by some as "the mistake of a lifetime," many buyers are reviewing reports that indicate the structural and mechanical integrity of properties they are considering buying.

[Since seeing the deplorable condition of your concrete work, the obvious attempts to cover up what appears to be a serious water problem in the basement, and hearing the noises emitted from your heating system and other appliances, I have decided that our office cannot place our sign in the yard until you have obtained a structural inspection and a mechanical inspection. On the other hand, since we are fast becoming friends, and I have yet to be sued, I thought I would recommend some additional cover-up procedures so that the problems are not evident to a prospective buyer. I will be moving out of the state by the end of the year anyway and just wanted to make one last fast commission first. Once the cover-up is completed, we will both keep the defects as our little secret so that you will always have something over on my broker and me.]

Having the requested information available when a prospective buyer inquires allows us a better chance of capturing a sale while other sellers are still trying to determine whether they will allow an inspection and at whose expense. While others are starting to bicker about who will select the various inspectors and the timing of the inspections, we will have the results available. This requires making a decision with regard to the type of inspection, the extent to which it will be performed, who will be selected to perform it and within what budget. Should any defects come to light, we will have the opportunity to make corrections or obtain adequate insurance before the discovery of some minor defect kills a potential sale.

Structural Inspection—Engineer's Report

Engineers are licensed by the state of Colorado. I am not and never want to be an engineer. As with all professions, the degree of expertise varies from individual to individual. If you have someone that you feel confident about, I would recommend you contact her soon. Most engineers will write a report indicating their opinion with regard to the structural integrity of the home in general. These professionals do not indicate the condition or life expectancy of the mechanical systems in your home. Although this can be expensive, it also is very useful to demonstrate to a prospective purchaser that a qualified expert has inspected the home. Sometimes it will discourage the buyer from obtaining his own inspection, which can save time and expense.

Mechanical Inspection—Home Warranty Companies

There are a number of companies offering a service which generally includes an inspection of the mechanical systems and appliances located in a home. The report will indicate whether they are in good working order and, should repair be necessary, what is suggested. In addition, these companies offer an insurance policy that protects the insured, usually the buyer, against failure of the indicated components within the terms of the policy. This may seem expensive; however, it is part of the marketing package included with a new home. New homes are definitely part of our competition.

There are numerous competitors in the marketplace for this kind of service. Although I cannot be responsible for the several individuals and companies listed on the attached sheet, I do know that they have been utilized before by other home owners. Each should be happy to provide you with a list of past clients to assist you in making your decision.

Although each policy needs to be read carefully, and the reputation of a company that issues such a policy be considered, I want to recommend only one particular entity since I will receive a fee if you select this company to write your insurance. This is just another attempt on my part to profit from your situation, and it provides my unknowing broker and me with an opportunity to be responsible for yet another possible liability involved in the sale of your home.

I will be happy to work with the professionals you select to provide access to your home, should you schedule their visit at a time when you will not be present. If you wish, after your selection and negotiation of the fee with the inspector, I will be glad to arrange for the actual timing of the inspection. Unless you indicate to the contrary, I will remain at your home until the inspection is complete.

Sincerely,
Denver Canadian Realty, Inc.

Daniel Mertz

by: Daniel Mertz, Agent

cc: Lee D. Weinstein, Broker

DENVER CANADIAN
REALTY, INC.
420 Ponderosa Drive   Boulder, CO 80303
(303) 494-6661

Mr. Gary S. Joiner
Mrs. Karen A. Joiner
4750 Table Mesa Drive
Boulder, CO 80303

    Re: 75 McCoy Drive, Windhaven

Dear Mr. and Mrs. Joiner:

As we discussed when I presented our company's policies prior to your selecting Denver Canadian Realty, Inc. and me to represent you, there are many outside factors that need to be determined or confirmed so that buyers can make informed decisions about what it is that they are buying. One of our objectives is that you complete the sale of your home without any lingering fears of later repercussions from the ultimate buyer, someone that you most probably do not even know yet.

While most people are inclined to inspect and review a property thoroughly before making an offer, some cautious buyers will want to have the property inspected for the presence of radon gas and other hazardous materials and to verify the condition of the soil prior to being obligated to purchase. Today many lenders and relocation companies make such verifications a must for their participation in a transaction.

As I indicated, the information that I have been reading suggests that all homes have some radon gas present. The key issue is to determine the amount. In addition, the composition of the soil on which the house is built concerns many buyers. In this area, bentonite, an expanding clay soil, is common. The key is to determine the composition of the soil, the extent to which it is composed of bentonite, whether or not the soil is a factor that needs to be addressed, and the extent of any hazardous substances, such as radon gas.

Most important, a potential purchaser will probably inquire about and subsequently require that a test be conducted prior to his final purchase of your home. All this takes time when you can least afford it, that is, after the buyer has bound your home with a signed contract but before the closing has occurred. This is a critical period when I like to have as few problems as possible.

The solution that we recommend is to have every home that we list tested as soon as possible for the condition of the soil and the presence and extent of radon gas and other hazardous materials. In this way, we can have the test results available for potential purchasers who can review them prior to making their decision to purchase and therefore hopefully eliminate the need for the contract to be conditional upon the results of a subsequent test.

A list of firms that provide these services is enclosed. Please talk it over, make a selection and order the tests. I would be glad to assist the tester of your choice by meeting her at the property during the day as I realize that you are both quite busy. In fact, after you make the selection and give me a budget of how much you wish to spend, I would be glad to arrange for the test on your behalf. Although everyone charges a different fee, we have found that the average is about $125 for the radon gas test and $135 for an engineer's report.

From my inspection of the home I could see no reason why both tests should not be simply a matter of course. Having them ready might just be the factor that helps that buyer decide on your home. Buyers, once they see what they want, usually are in a hurry to move in. The inspections would eliminate one more delay.

As I mentioned on my initial meeting with you, there are a number of areas that would tend to indicate to a potential purchaser that the property has some form of structural defect. Once this is known to me I have to point out the presence of such a defect. Having an engineer's report to show that the repairs you have elected to perform will totally take care of the potential problem, or that you have already performed the repairs satisfactorily to eliminate the problem will help market what otherwise could be a slower moving property.

When you have made your selection, just indicate it on the bottom of this letter and drop it back to my office. I have enclosed a stamped self-addressed envelope for your convenience. Thank you for selecting me as your agent. I like your home and enjoy stating that we are your agents. I know you want to complete this sale with a minimum of delay and potential problems. Therefore I am willing to do whatever you direct to expedite that and to coordinate the people you choose to make the necessary repairs and inspections.

Sincerely,
Denver Canadian Realty, Inc.

James C. Smittkamp

by: James C. Smittkamp, Agent

Enc. List of Radon Inspectors
     List of Soils Engineers

DENVER CANADIAN REALTY, INC.

Direction to Obtain Inspections

Jim, please consider this as my instruction to contact and employ on my behalf the indicated inspectors that I have selected, at the rates indicated, to inspect my property and present a written report as soon as possible. Please make sure that the mechanical inspector presents an estimate of the premium for a Home Warranty Policy for a one-year period.

Engineer: _____

Upper Fee Limit: $ _____ Phone: _____

Mechanical Inspector: _____

Limit on Fees: _____ Phone: _____

Radon Inspector: _____

Limit on Fees: _____ Phone: _____

I hereby authorize and direct you to present the results of all inspections to any and all prospective purchasers. This will help to eliminate any potential liability either of us might incur. Please indicate to each inspector that he should send the statement for his services directly to me for payment. Thank you for your efforts.

Gary S. Joiner
Gary S. Joiner

This type of request can be used for almost anything and is often included at the bottom of a letter. The return of the letter not only indicates authorization for the services to be performed at the seller's expense through the people the seller has selected, but also confirms the receipt by the seller of the other terms in the letter.

Confirming Action

DENVER CANADIAN
REALTY, INC.
420 Ponderosa Drive   Boulder, CO 80303
(303) 494-6661

Mrs. and Mr. Gary S. Joiner
4750 Table Mesa Drive
Boulder, CO 80303

    Re: 75 McCoy Drive, Windhaven
       Inspector Selection

Dear Gary and Karen:

It was nice to get your call today. This is just a note to tell you that I was able to contact Jim Rodgers and he agreed to complete the engineer's report within the next two weeks for a fee not to exceed $150. In addition, I also contacted Mike J. Miller of Radon Gas Associates and told him that he could come over next Thursday to perform the test for the flat fee you agreed with him on of $125.

I compliment you on your selection of experts for inspections. I am happy that I was able to obtain their services within the budget you set. I do not want to spend any more of your money than absolutely necessary. Both specialists indicated that they would bill you directly at the end of the job.

One more step to a well-planned sale. It never ceases to amaze me what it takes to properly market a property in these complicated times. If you have any questions please give me a call. It is a pleasure to act as your listing agent. I hope that your wife is feeling better.

                Sincerely,
                Denver Canadian Realty, Inc.

                James C. Smittkamp

                by: Jim Smittkamp, Agent

cc: Lee D. Weinstein, Broker

DENVER CANADIAN
REALTY, INC.
420 Ponderosa Drive   Boulder, CO 80303
(303) 494-6661

Mr. Gary S. Joiner
Mrs. Karen A. Joiner
4750 Table Mesa Drive
Boulder, CO 80303

    Re: 75 McCoy Drive, Windhaven

Dear Mr. and Mrs. Joiner:

    As I indicated, upon listing your home we want to start the procedure to get it into the MLS system as soon as possible. Enclosed is the input form that I have completed for your home. Please review it as soon as possible so that I can get it submitted to the Multiple Listing Service. If you desire to change or correct anything let me or Janine at the front desk know immediately as we are eager to accurately represent your home and get it into the system as fast as possible. Unless there are a lot of changes, a phone call will do the job nicely. I know you are busy and if I do not hear to the contrary by January 15, 1991, I will assume that everything is correct and will submit the Listing Information as is to the MLS next Friday.

    Your home shows so nicely that I think an open house might be a good marketing tool to employ. We would be present at all times and advertise in advance to attract people who might like to see your home without the formality of a scheduled appointment. Please let me know if that is acceptable to you. It is a good time to take a day off and let me [an agent from this office] sit in your home. There is always someone present to insure the integrity of your home.

    As I indicated, one of the available marketing tools to allow fast access to other cooperating and in-house salespersons is to place a lock box on your door. This is a combination box that contains a key to your home and is accessed by a code that we can and do change periodically. The code for your home would be assigned and changed by our office and not the same as any other codes currently used by our firm. Please read the Lock Box Authorization Form and sign and return it to me if you wish to utilize this system. Note that you can elect to limit the use of the combination as indicated by the various options.

I look forward to showing your home off to the entire office next Tuesday when your home is scheduled as part of our weekly office tour. It is so nice to have my name on your property listing. If you have any questions, please feel free to call me or my broker Evelyn M. Ruka at any time.

Most Sincerely,
Denver Canadian Realty, Inc.

James C. Smittkamp

by: James C. Smittkamp, Agent

cc: Evelyn M. Ruka, Broker

DENVER CANADIAN REALTY, INC.

Lock Box Authorization Form

We, the undersigned owners of the following described real estate, hereby authorize you, Denver Canadian Realty, Inc., subject to the indicated conditions, to place a lock box on our door. We fully understand that the combination will be set by you and changed by you at intervals you determine. In addition, we understand that you will not be responsible or liable to us for the unauthorized use of the lock box or the key located therein, so long as you are in compliance with the terms of this agreement. We understand that potential subagents will contact you and request the combination which you are authorized to provide to them so that they can view our property without you in attendance. We realize that there is a risk that the combination will be discovered by parties with interests adverse to ours and that it may encourage people to consider this property for illegal entry.

Property Address: _____

Type of Lock Box: _____

Special Conditions: _____

_____

Dated: _____

Owners: Denver Canadian Realty, Inc.

_____   by: *James C. Smittkamp*
                                           James C. Smittkamp, Agent

_____

Liability for the Premises

The Key

The seller usually gives the agent a key to the house. This starts a series of delegations of the right to enter the property. The number of reported thefts and other problems grow as the agents become more involved in the servicing of many different listings and the touring of houses with various buyers. The mere fact that a person has obtained a real estate license and possibly joined a board is unfortunately no indication of the reputation, degree of care, integrity, or ability of that agent. More important, the customers of some brokers, unknown to those agents, use this showing procedure as an opportunity to case vacant houses and view possible entry systems or to set up open windows or doors for accomplices. There are even some subagents that let the purchaser have the key to view the property. You needn't worry your client with all these particulars. But keep them well in mind yourself so that you will always remember to help your client understand his or her side of the responsibility inherent in letting others into the home. Be clear and be safe.

Buyers' Brokers

If the person requesting the showing is a buyer's broker, assume that you need a higher degree of concern and care. This should be paramount in the listing broker's mind, and the decision to allow an unaccompanied showing should be more closely examined. The broker is becoming responsible for the manner in which he protects the property of his client, the seller. Ask yourself: "Could I demonstrate a high degree of care in court? To whom did I give the key or the lock box combination? Was it someone who identified herself as an agent, not of the seller but for a buyer? Was it to someone I did not even know?"

Personal Unlocking Service

There is absolutely no substitute for opening the home for each prospective purchaser, whether or not accompanied by any other form of agent. This does not suggest interfering with the relationship between the prospective purchaser and the agent showing that prospective purchaser the home. There is an absolute duty to take care of the house when you get the key and a responsibility to insure that others who acquire entry to the house and/or use of the key be scrutinized carefully. Remember: It is very easy to make a duplicate key. Decide how much of the risk you can reasonably accept and let your client know your limits.

Expensive Items—Limit of Liability

The seller is someone that you know very little about and who may have an insurance claim in mind for items that were never on the property. Establish the extent of liability and the degree of care that is expected. In addition, ask the seller to make an inventory of expensive items. Simply and politely state that the firm is not responsible for furs, jewelry, gun collections and the like. Recommend that the seller temporarily store these items elsewhere during the marketing of the home.

The Lock Box

Various lock boxes, which can vary from the rudimentary, single key for everyone in the board—a bad system currently still used by some groups of real estate people and also used by HUD—to the combination lock box (utilizing a combination other than "SPY"), to the ultimate in modern sophisticated computer systems are all currently available. Great care should be taken in the selection of a system and in giving access to the key, combination or code. Not even the cover letter will protect you from the negligence of your own agents nor that of the plethora of subagents waiting to see or preview the house for whatever reason.

Nothing protects you from gross negligence, such as the giving out of the lock box combination to unknown persons assumed to be real estate agents, or the dissemination of the information over the car phone. Neither the firm nor the agent should have a standard combination. Be demonstrably cautious. Never use the same combination for more than one property at any given point in time. Change the combination between listings, and certainly see that the combination be changed at least monthly, if not weekly. A lock box authorization or release form is a must.

Case in Point

The owner of a condominium in a large complex allows the agent to put the key to the entire building in a lock box placed on the main entry. There is a theft, and the broker is held responsible for encouraging the thief by the placement of the lock box, indicating that a vacant unit in the building is for sale. To make matters worse, the agent also placed a lock box on the unit entry door. This was a nice way of pointing to the unit that was for sale and, in the mind of at least one hearing panel member, of making the unit vulnerable. That was held to be negligence since there was a theft in the unit for sale and in two other units in the building in a single day.

Interestingly enough there was no accurate record of the individuals who had access to the combination nor of those who had shown the property in the preceding two weeks. The few names that were available proved to include one person that was not a member of any board, held no license, and had no operable local phone number.

The listed unit was robbed without the use of force. It is so easy when you have the combination. I wonder what a court would have decided. The broker was very happy to write a few checks.

Periodic Inventory

If there are a lot of valuable items left in a listed home, a periodic inventory by the seller and/or agent may help to eliminate the allegations of negligence or theft that may arise in such situations. Some people, after claiming that they were robbed while the property was listed, have been extremely lucky in their post-theft, post-settlement with some insurance company to be able to locate items almost identical to those that were stolen. There is no need to be a victim of such practices.

DENVER CANADIAN
REALTY, INC.
420 Ponderosa Drive   Boulder, CO 80303
(303) 494-6661

Mr. Gary S. Joiner
Mrs. Karen A. Joiner
4750 Table Mesa Drive
Boulder, CO 80303

    Re: 75 McCoy Drive, Windhaven

Dear Mr. and Mrs. Joiner:

There are several methods for showing your home. Our preferred method is for any agent outside our office to have an opportunity to talk with Jim or me prior to any showings. We make this known to every agent dealing with a prospective purchaser, whether that agent be a buyer's broker or a subagent. This is not always possible, however, and sometimes the agent on duty or our receptionist describes the home and its important features to the other agent prior to a showing.

Once the showing has been completed, we contact the other agent for a report. Although it is impossible to know all of the possible subagents that might show your home personally, we will not let anyone unknown to us show your home unaccompanied. We have informed all other prospective subagents that we reserve the right to accompany anyone who displays an interest in viewing your home.

In spite of all our efforts, we feel that it is always in your best interests to place valuable jewelry, coins, currency, and other easily-removable items in your safety deposit box at your bank or to store these items, as well as expensive tools and furs and the like, at another location. We simply cannot and will not be responsible for such items. If you have any items of value, other than your ordinary furniture, such as expensive televisions, computers, video equipment and the like, we encourage you to mark these items with your social security number and to provide us with an inventory and relative value statement. We have included a simple form given us by the Farmer's Insurance Agency to assist you in taking such an inventory. Unless we receive an inventory, we cannot be responsible for any items left in your home during this marketing period.

If you desire, we will place a lock box on your home. This presents special risks for the unauthorized entry to your home and requires your written authorization prior to its placement. The advantage of having a key placed in the lock box is that other agents can, after making a telephone appointment, view the home without the need to travel to several offices to obtain keys and then having to repeat the journey after each series of showings. In a metro area such as ours, the distance between offices can be great. If your home is easy to see, thus saving the potential subagents time and travel, it will probably receive more showings.

It is our policy to change the combination weekly to avoid the unauthorized use of the combination. Please complete the lock box approval form included with this letter if you desire to utilize that system.

With a house that is as nice as yours or that has a location such as yours, we have found that having it open to the public on a Saturday, Sunday or evening gives people an opportunity to look through your home in a relaxed atmosphere. Warm bread in the oven, a fire in the fireplace or cut flowers can enhance the sense that your home is perfect for them. We would have an agent on the premises at all times and would encourage you to take the day off and go somewhere else so that the house is available for inspection by interested persons. This allows the home to look larger and more spacious than it would if we were all there and also reduces the intimidation factor when a prospective purchaser enters. I will be contacting you to schedule some tentative times so that I can plan an advertising strategy in advance to try to maximize the number of prospects we can anticipate.

Thank you again for listing your home with our agency. We are happy to be marketing your property for you.

Most sincerely,
Denver Canadian Realty, Inc.

James C. Smittkamp

by: James C. Smittkamp, Broker

cc: Lee D. Weinstein, Broker

Property Management

By Design

Property management seems to flow from two distinct sources. First, the arrangement is set up by design. The owner and the agent enter into a comprehensive agreement dealing with the rights, duties, and obligations of both the owner and the agent. These vary from simple rent collection and mortgage payment application, to full rental and management authority, including the right to offer, negotiate and lease the premises, bring eviction actions, contract and pay for repairs, and generally deal with the real property.

By Default

Second, a property management arrangement simply happens. This occurs when the real estate professional, while in the course of her normal listing duties, is called upon to be the agent for the owner in a capacity not anticipated or delineated in the original listing agreement. The agent then unwittingly becomes a more comprehensive agent for the owner for leasing, repair, maintenance, eviction, and so forth without the proper agreement. The result is that the owner denies the relationship when it suits him and the agent and broker are left with expenses, tenant suits, and other problems without any assistance from the owner. See to it early that your duties are made clear so that you will not be victimized by either an owner's exaggerated expectations or by your own desire to be helpful.

Confirmation of the Tenancy

If you should decide to accept the job of property manager, I would suggest a nice little letter to each tenant to verify the current status of that particular tenant's tenancy. This will serve to verify the information given you by the landlord, if in fact you were so lucky as to get any information, and establish a rapport with the tenants. This type of letter can also be useful at the start of a new year just so that the tenant does not start to feel he is the owner.

Eviction

There are those that need excitement in the world and eviction is the place to get it. If you are going to act as the agent for the eviction of a tenant, I would recommend a series of cover letters to confirm each step in the procedure and to request instructions often. When the counterclaim comes it will be nice to be able to hide under the agency cloak. To be entitled to that protection, you must have been acting within the scope of your agency. Yes, that means more than a standard listing agreement.

Tenant Mentality

Tenants are important people in real estate. It is the tenant and his all-important rental payments that drive the income property market. The good tenants can mean a lot and deserve an owner's best. But recognize that many tenants are red flags. These others fit part of our plaintiff profile. They do not generally have a lot of assets, wish they owned a house, are jealous of the owner and his real estate agent, have little down-side risk in litigation, and very often no ability to stick around after you win the suit, let alone pay the amount of the judgment against them. I have yet to recover from a tenant, in court, what it has cost me to play.

Yes, your principles are important. But just as with the other kind of principal, they need to be placed where they will compound interest, not compound problems. If, for whatever reason, you must function as a manager, get a written agreement and get paid separately and adequately for it.

Protection

As the broker and/or agent you are interested in protecting yourself from the perils and pitfalls of becoming a volunteer management agent. At the same time you want to keep the listing and assist the owner as much as necessary so that the property can be marketed. At first this may seem impossible, but it is really quite easy. All that is required is that you define the relationship as it exists and as it may evolve.

It is important to note that property management is not covered by many of the professional liability insurers. This is because of the extreme exposure and loss that occurs in this field when it is practiced by the inexperienced real estate agent, generally without any documentation as to the extent of the agent's authority. A quick review of your policy might be helpful.

Tenancy Agreements

The tendency to suggest or use a lease agreement that was used in the last deal or is a standard form can be very strong. Resist the urge. Have the owner select and designate a form. Do not proffer your form; that is the practice of law and not necessary to accomplish the objective. Leases, even in the most mundane residential transaction, are very complex and often devoid of what might later prove to be important clauses.

Timing

As with all notices and agreements, agreement before the fact is the preferred route. In this case, however, the memorandum of previous oral conversation or agreement, discussed earlier in this book, is a useful bootstrapping tool. If you sense that any of your relationships might be cloudy on this matter, fire off some memorandums of your previous oral agreements or conversations immediately.

Payment

You work hard enough to earn your normal commission. Charge a fee for the additional management services you may be induced to perform. Fees are a good way to either eliminate the request for management or to open the door for a satisfactory comprehensive management agreement.

Withdrawal

Any management agreement—in addition to a multitude of other agreements not to be discussed in this book— should contain a provision allowing you to withdraw, turn the damage deposits over to the owner, with tenant confirmation of course, and stop managing the property when you have had enough.

DENVER CANADIAN
REALTY, INC.
420 Ponderosa Drive   Boulder, CO 80303
(303) 494-6661

Mr. and Mrs. Robert S. Caplan
750 Prospect Lane
Colorado Springs, CO 80903

Re: Unit 203 B

Dear Mr. and Mrs. Caplan:

Please let this letter serve to introduce me as the new manager for the owner of this building. I enjoy assisting people with their living needs and want you to know that I am available during normal working hours at the above office. Please feel free to contact me there for the payment of rent and other business related to the building. I too have a family and have promised my wife that I will not work after 5:00 P.M. unless it is an emergency. I know you will understand that in an emergency I would want you by all means to contact me at home at 494-4664.

[Let me introduce myself. In order to obtain the listing for the sale of the building where you are now a tenant, I have grudgingly decided to manage the property. Please refrain from making statements that would hinder the sale of the property as I am showing it at odd hours of the day and night. The only reason that I am taking this job is that I hope it will help me retain the listing on the property.]

My records indicate that the following is a correct status report of your account:

Your family consists of:
Robert, Laurian, Monica and Adam
No pets are allowed

Monthly rent: $450.00   Deposit: $475.00
Rent is due on the: 1st   Late on the: 15th
Rent is paid in advance   Late Charge: $50.00
Rent paid through: March

If this is incorrect please call me and send me a written letter indicating what you feel is in error. You must do both. If it is easier, just make a notation on this letter and sign your name. If I do not hear from you to the contrary, I will understand that this is the correct information.

Sincerely,
Denver Canadian Realty, Inc.

Lee D. Weinstein

by: Lee D. Weinstein, Broker

cc: Fubico of America, Inc.

Property Management

DENVER CANADIAN
REALTY, INC.
420 Ponderosa Drive   Boulder, CO 80303
(303) 494-6661

Mr. and Mrs. Gary S. Joiner
4750 Table Mesa Drive
Boulder, CO 80303

    Re: Property Management
       75 McCoy Drive, Windhaven

Dear Mr. and Mrs. Joiner:

Thank you for telling me that you will be moving out by the end of the month. I had hoped that your home would sell by this time. I know that you intend to rent the property for a few months on a month-to-month basis and thought I should explain the firm's position with regard to our property management services.

[As I indicated to you earlier, neither Denver Canadian, Inc., nor any of its agents are allowed to engage in the property management business. Our broker feels that we are in the business of representing sellers and in the professional marketing of our clients' homes for sale (as well as representing buyers interested in the purchase of real estate), and not in the management of real property. It can be very time-consuming and can distract us from our primary goal. I wish I could help you, but it is simply not possible. There are a lot of people who do nothing but property management, a list of those people can be furnished to you if you need a place to start. Often a friend or neighbor is adequate for the isolated short-term case.]

[In response to your request, let me outline the services we are happy to provide for our sellers with regard to the management of their property.] Property that is occupied by people other than the owner often raises the concern about the extent of management that the owner may expect from us as listing agents.

Property management is not covered in the standard [state-approved] listing contract, and, therefore, we do not render any property management services without the express prior written approval of the owner. We have long felt that the listing of a property for sale and the management of real estate are very different tasks and should be covered separately.

Since your property is currently rented, let me take a brief moment to explain our services for owners that are also landlords. We have two types of agency relationships available in the property management field.

First, our limited service. Under this plan, we do not take an active role in the management of the property. We limit ourselves to responding to your instructions, preferably in letter form, requesting us to accomplish certain specific tasks. Such items include: the collecting of rents, paying specific payments, arranging for work to be done or confirming that the work has in fact been performed, showing the property to prospective tenants, cooperating with the attorney of your selection—in the event eviction becomes necessary—and generally working on a case-by-case basis with no duty to manage the property, except as indicated.

Our fee for this service is included in our standard listing commission as we try hard to do as much work for nothing as possible while still exposing ourselves to as much liability as possible. This liability is particularly attractive as it does not even require that we earn a fee. Should your property not sell for any reason—not to mention our selection of tenants or overall management skills—you do not have to pay us anything, and, therefore, the property management was just another attempt to attract litigation without compensation. This is definitely what sets us apart from the competition.

Second is our full-service management service. This is the subject of our Management and Agency Agreement, a copy of which is enclosed for your review. We would be happy to provide you with full-service management. Before we can accept the responsibility of full-service management, this agreement needs to be completed, signed both by you as owner and by the broker, and returned to the office with the indicated retainer deposit of $500.

As you can see, the full-service management agreement provides that we will use our best efforts to lease, maintain, supervise, and care for your property on your behalf. This involves much more than simply collecting the rents and doing as you indicate; therefore, it is the subject of a separate, comprehensive, agreement.

Unless we receive your written selection of the method of service that you desire, we will assume that we are not responsible for the management and maintenance of the property. Should you direct us to perform certain tasks, we will assume that we are operating under the provisions outlined above under the first option.

Fees for the management of property, outlined above, are separate from the commission that we earn by acting as your listing agents for the sale for your property. Unless otherwise agreed in writing, we will charge you for our management services on an hourly basis. Brokers' and salespersons' time will be calculated at $45.00 per hour, and support people's time will be calculated at $30.00 per hour. We reserve the right to designate the person we feel is best suited to perform the indicated tasks.

In addition, when we start to perform service, there is a setup fee of $50.00 to open the management account. All billings will be monthly, and in the event of nonpayment, we will deduct the amount past due from your retainer and consider such nonpayment as direction to stop the work that we are performing. Should you wish us to contract for services of other third parties, we will do so in your name only. Since these services are in the nature of improvement to the property, we consider ourselves as being covered by the mechanic's lien statutes of Colorado.

Equity Skimming

Although this does not apply to our property management business nor to your ideas for the management of property, I feel that it is nice to know the overall meaning of the term "equity skimming" so that neither of us is confused with those who are utilizing this tactic. In this situation, the owner, intending from the outset to make money and not payments, acquires a property with the present intent to rent it and keep the rent paid by the tenants. Such a person does not pay the utility companies, the taxes, the association fees, nor the mortgage payments. It is important to note that intent is a key element in this definition.

Equity skimming is not a term that would generally apply to the owner of a single property who, after owning it for some time, finds that she can no longer subsidize the rent to make all the required payments. To avoid even the appearance of impropriety in circumstances where we, in our own discretion, feel that such is the case, we will not release any money to the owner unless we are satisfied that it is being applied to the payment of the utilities, association dues, the mortgage and the like, and that all such payments are being made in full.

Finally, we will resign immediately from any property management functions, in situations which we, in our sole discretion, determine may be considered by some as "equity skimming." I know this will not be a problem with your property. We just want to be sure that all agents explain the firm policy to all our clients.

Thank you for your consideration of our property management services. As you can see, this is a very different part of the real estate business and it operates under different rules. We would be happy to provide you with these services at your request. As always, if I can be of any further assistance, please do not hesitate to let me know. We are proud to have your property listed for sale with this office and feel that we can complete the marketing of your real estate with or without regard to our being part of the property's management.

Most sincerely,
Denver Canadian Realty, Inc.

James C. Smittkamp

by: Jim Smittkamp, Sales Agent

cc: Evelyn M. Ruka, Broker

Termination of a Listing and Postlisting Period Protection

In order to protect yourself under the terms of the Listing Agreement, you must disclose the names of all persons with whom you have negotiated for the sale of the property during the listing period. Note that a showing is not a requirement, only negotiations. Contrary to some opinions, the presentation of a contract from a prospective purchaser during the listing period does satisfy this requirement. Note that the disclosure of the list of parties must also be made during the listing period. Written disclosures are all that we are concerned with here since a seller is unlikely to acknowledge an oral disclosure if there is litigation.

Under current law you do not have any right to a lien, *Lis Pendens*, or other form of prejudgment attachment upon the property or the proceeds of a pending sale for any sums that are due as a result of the listing agreement. Yours is a personal services contract.

The difficult task is to protect yourself with regard to the negotiations conducted with prospective purchasers by your subagents because they will generally not have disclosed the names of their customers to you. This is where a good record of showings and interest in the property will allow you to contact those subagents and request that they provide you with the needed information. Some people feel that it is the duty of such a subagent to provide that information in a timely manner. Those same people might even consider a refusal that resulted in the loss of a commission as a basis for litigation.

Try to impress upon the seller the complexity of the sale of real estate today so that the seller will feel that he truly does need your services even if someone were to approach him the day after the expiration of the listing. The letter to the seller should attempt to emphasize some facet of the transaction you feel he is most uncomfortable with, such as sources of new financing, the need to accept a home in trade, or a guaranteed sale, the need for a home warranty program, or other service that he cannot get form the local attorney who probably has no idea how to market a home properly anyway. That attorney will be your competition once the buyer is located.

You may have a noncontractual claim for a commission if you can show you were the procuring cause of an ultimate sale. Do not place too much faith in this or other "equitable" remedies. The success of those claims has generally been in the absence of a listing contract. When there is a contract, the court will look to it for the agreement of the parties.

DENVER CANADIAN
REALTY, INC.
420 Ponderosa Drive   Boulder, CO 80303
(303) 494-6661

Mr. David A. Farus, Broker
SunWest Realty and Insurance, Inc.
45 West Plaza Street
Denver, Colorado 80909

    Re: 75 McCoy Drive, Windhaven

Dear Dave:

    Our records indicate that you scheduled and completed a showing of the above referenced property. While I think that the sellers will renew their listing with this office, I like to try to protect all of the brokers who have acted as our subagents during the listing period, should one of their buyers ultimately purchase the property and, with or without the knowledge and assistance of the seller, attempt to avoid paying us our commission, which would eliminate your being paid your portion of such an earned commission. To try to avoid such a result, I need to indicate to the seller the names of those individuals you may have negotiated with or have shown the property to and the dates of your negotiations and/or showings.

    I understand that you may be reluctant to provide us with that information for fear that we will then try to sell other listings to those individuals you have indicated to us are interested in buying this listing. I can assure you that we will not attempt to solicit your customers. There is simply no reason for us both to lose the right to an earned commission. If you want to discuss this matter with me personally, please call me immediately. Otherwise, please leave the list of names and supporting information in the form of a message with Evelyn to be followed up by a letter. Time is short and your cooperation is greatly appreciated.

    Thank you for your assistance. In the event you ever need the same assistance from this office upon the expiration of one of your listings, please do not hesitate to ask and we will comply promptly. We are competitors, but there is no need to allow a seller to profit from our failure to protect ourselves as the standard listing provides.

I look forward to working with you in the future, appreciate you as a competitor and further appreciate your association with us and your attempts to market this property.

Most sincerely,
Denver Canadian Realty, Inc.

Lee D. Weinstein

by: Lee D. Weinstein, Broker

DENVER CANADIAN
REALTY, INC.
420 Ponderosa Drive   Boulder, CO 80303
(303) 494-6661

Mr. Gary S. Joiner
Mrs. Karen A. Joiner
4750 Table Mesa Drive
Boulder, CO 80303

    Re: 75 McCoy Drive, Windhaven

Dear Mr. and Mrs. Joiner:

In spite of all of our efforts, our listing period is about to expire. Your property has been a pleasure to show, and we have been happy to receive so many nice compliments from the numerous cooperating brokers who have had the opportunity to show your home. Your efforts to accommodate our attempts and your willingness to always have your house ready for last-minute showings have certainly been helpful. We all want to commend you on your efforts.

Try as we have, we seem to have been unable to locate a buyer who is ready, willing, and able to complete the purchase of your home as proposed in your instructions in the Listing Agreement. Jim will be contacting you to encourage you to relist the property with this firm. We are all very eager to locate a suitable buyer for you. Jim and the rest of us know your home better than anyone else and have invested quite a lot of time and money in the marketing of your home. We have enjoyed the cooperation of several of the other brokers and appreciate their efforts on behalf of both of us.

The following is a list of the persons that we or our subagents have been negotiating with and who have not yet made an acceptable offer to purchase your home. Should any of these individuals purchase your home during the postlisting period indicated in the Listing Agreement, they would be considered to have been located and procured through our efforts. We therefore would be entitled to payment of the commission indicated in the Listing Agreement. If one of these parties desires to purchase your home, we would be happy to assist you in the sale and complete the transaction by extending the listing for such a purchaser.

As always, the sale of your home on terms acceptable to you is our primary concern. We hope that some of these people do in fact purchase your home within the allotted time since it will accomplish your goals and help us to recover the expenses we have incurred in our efforts to market your home, including exposing it to the other brokers that are members of the Multiple Listing Service.

Prospective purchasers obtained directly through this office:

Mr. Peter Walters
Mr. Bill Henderson
Mr. and Mrs. Randall Kemp
Mr. Gary J. Caswell

In addition, the following subagents have shown the property and have negotiated on your behalf with their customers:

Mr. Alexander Swift, A. Swift and Company
Mrs. Monica Jean Wilson, The Langley Coach Company

[Including only brokers is risky but may assist you in trying to collect. It would be better to have their customers' names.] Often the basis for the ultimate decision to purchase begins with the introduction to the property by one of our agents or subagents, but there is simply not enough time to bring the buyer to the final decision prior to the expiration of the listing. Should any of these buyers contact you, please give me a call immediately so that I can complete the sale in a professional manner. With real estate being as complicated as it is today, there is a lot more to be done than just drafting a contract for sale if the seller is to be properly represented and the buyer made aware of the different sources of financing that are available.

Thank you for allowing us the opportunity to market your home. I trust you will relist with Jim when he meets with you. If there is anything I can do to assist you or clarify our position, please do not hesitate to call me.

Most sincerely,
Denver Canadian Realty, Inc.

by: Lee D. Weinstein, Broker

Listing Agreement Clauses

Although this is not a forms manual for completing a Listing Agreement, it seems like a logical place to include some ideas for clauses that pertain to the items discussed in this book. As usual, try to determine not only what will transpire but also who will be in charge of making decisions.

Assuming that all contracts have provisions advising the parties to seek competent legal counsel, I will not deal with that alternative.

You may want to include some of the following items, modified to fit your particular circumstances, as appropriate:

Dual Agency Possibility

In addition to our representation of your property and the properties of other sellers we also do the following: represent and act as agents for buyers under the terms of a buyer's-broker agreement, have agents within our office who may have an interest in your property for their own account, understand that agents within the firm may have clients who have listed their property with this firm as you have done and who are interested in your property. In the event that such people should show an interest in your property and choose to make an offer to purchase your property, the following shall apply:

a. We shall, if it is known to us, indicate to you that the buyer has a potential conflict of interest, the nature of the potential conflict, and that the buyer may have had access to confidential information about the property and your financial condition as you have so indicated the same to this firm.

b. We shall not be responsible for any loss sustained by you or anyone else which is the result of an offer, contract, closing or otherwise, which is related to, or results from, any interest of such a buyer in your property.

c. We shall not be obligated to inform anyone of—even though we may know about—the financial qualifications or otherwise with regard to the buyer. We will endeavor to stop the flow of information between the parties but will not be responsible in any way for any such flow of information.

d. The compensation portion of our agreement will not be altered by any such occurrence.

Should you desire that we not encourage the types of individuals indicated above to take an interest in your property, please so indicate by deleting this portion of the listing agreement and initialing your deletion.

(What I sometimes think is the real intent follows:)

a. We shall not be responsible to indicate to you any information that we have obtained about the financial qualifications of the buyer, his personal traits, the amount that we feel he will pay in the event you decide to counter any offer the buyer might present or otherwise pursue. Oh yes, we will still want to be paid in full the agreed-upon commission as your agents.

b. We will of course give you any confidential information that we have as to the extent of the needs, financial depth, price and terms that we feel the buyer would be willing to offer to purchase your property. In other words, all the secrets that we have obtained from the buyer in confidence would be told to you to help you obtain the best possible price for your home from this buyer who, until he selected your home, was our principal. Of course, we would never disclose to the buyer your bottom price, last counteroffer price or personal financial position.

c. In short, sometimes we like him better, sometimes we like you better. All we want to do is put the deal together and get paid. *C'est la vie*.

FHA Mortgage Insurance Premiums

Prepaid FHA mortgage insurance premiums shall be prorated to the date of delivery of deed using the schedule attached to this Listing Agreement.

The unused portion of any prepaid FHA mortgage insurance premiums will be purchased by the buyer at closing. The amount will be determined [by Cindy Trautwein of Trautwein Title and Abstract using whatever tables or charts she deems appropriate] by utilizing the attached tables provided by HUD for this purpose.

Hazard Insurance

Broker has advised the seller that his existing hazard insurance policy may not cover the period of time between the closing and delivery of deed and the actual surrender of possession by the seller. The seller is advised to seek the counsel of his insurance agent and obtain a written assurance satisfactory to the seller as to the extent of his coverage on and after closing.

Seller is hereby advised that in the event he allows someone other than himself to occupy the property, either during the pendency of the listing or after the sale has closed, the existing hazard insurance policy may not cover the premises or the possessions of the seller or the occupant.

Liability Upon Assumption

Seller acknowledges that the broker has explained the following:

The seller, in the absence of a written release signed by the lender to the contrary, will remain liable for the repayment of the loan on the property in the event the seller allows it to be assumed. In the event of an assumption, the seller may be unable to reacquire the property should the loan go into default or foreclosure.

The broker, her agents, subagents and employees are not liable for any event that occurs after the delivery of the deed, including, but not limited to, a failure on the part of the buyer or the assigns of the buyer to make any payments after assuming the mortgage or after a subsequent transfer without an assumption. We are not responsible for the actions of the buyer after the property is transferred.

Owner acknowledges that, although a purchaser may assume the existing note and deed of trust [mortgage], the owner shall personally remain liable for the ultimate repayment of the loan.

The seller understands that the broker is purchasing the property and not assuming the loan. The buyer, who is also the broker, is not personally obligated for the ultimate repayment of the loan while you the seller remain liable for its repayment. In the event the broker sells the property to another buyer, even if that buyer should assume the loan, the broker shall not be responsible for the subsequent buyer's or any other buyer's performance or lack thereof. [This is just a guaranteed sale, designed to divest you of title while leaving you personally responsible for the payments, and the broker is unwilling to be responsible for the repayment of the loan for the rest of time.] This is not a conflict of interest, the broker is just trying to protect himself at your expense.

Schedule of Rents and Deposits

The owner warrants that the attached schedule of rents and deposits is a true and correct representation of the rents and deposits actually collected and currently due. In addition, the owner represents that each individual listed as a tenant is actually occupying the property according to the terms indicated. Owner shall transfer all deposits and prorate all rents as of the date of delivery of deed. There are no incentives in effect. [that would alter or amend the rental information contained on the attached list.]

Title Insurance Form 130

Seller agrees to cooperate with the reasonable requests of a purchaser to execute all documents reasonably required by the designated title insurance company, including Lien Affidavits, and to allow the property to be surveyed and inspected in order for the purchaser to obtain a Form 130 endorsement to the title insurance policy, so long as these items are at the sole expense of the purchaser.

Chapter Three

Dealing with Buyers

General Information

The Nature of Buyers

1. Buyers are the ones who will own the property that you are currently trying to market. As owners, then, they may soon become sellers and potential clients.

2. Buyers will be around after the sale and will remember who helped them acquire this new piece of real estate. Although you may represent the seller, it is the buyer who will probably either sue you or start a suit you will get to participate in, if the buyer feels that there is a chance of victory and reward.

3. Buyers that are dissatisfied with their new acquisition will be looking for a way to get out of the deal. Resale is no longer the easy answer since inflation has all but disappeared. The only other easy mark is you.

4. Sellers, lacking a seller-financing situation, will generally have their money and be gone, sometimes out of state, and as a practical matter may not be available to help with the postclosing problems. They often do not remember the key points that were so easy to express only months before.

5. Buyer representation is a modern concern, both for the industry and for the court system. Whether or not your company allows such a system, and there are many arguments for and against offering it as an alternative, it must either be explained or you must indicate clearly that you are a seller's subagent. Everyone must understand the concept of a buyer agency and be prepared to deal with it in some fashion, either as an acceptable alternative or not, as the company policy may be.

Passive Defense Techniques.

1. It is always nice to have someone in a lawsuit who has the ability to pay. Attorneys call this the "deep pocket" theory. Be the poorest in the group.

2. Wealth is a personal thing. There is no need to explain to potential plaintiffs that you have a lot of money.

3. The perception that you are not much of an adversary, are poorly organized, do not to pay attention to details, do not keep good records, have something to hide—such as a transaction that did not fit the rules— may encourage someone to include you in a legal action.

4. Try not to discuss other transactions that you have completed in order to indicate that a risky transaction will work. The more you describe other transactions, the more you may have the opportunity to defend a tenuous perception of what happened.

5. Display the image of an organized, detail-oriented, highly professional agent who always follows the rules and is above reproach. Be someone who does not make a derogatory comment about others.

6. Always try to limit the amount of information you give to a buyer, client, or other potential plaintiff.

7. Limit your liability by explaining alternatives, rules, local sources of information, the extent of your abilities, and agency status in written form early on.

Discovery

Being shown is not the same as discovering something for yourself. No matter what your agency relationship, be a provider of the kind of information that lets the buyer discover things and make independent informed decisions. There is ultimately only one judge for the buyer, and that is the buyer. Everyone tries to place the apparent decision-making authority on someone else. We all hope that someone else will decide for us. Deep inside, however, we make our own decisions and are doing exactly what we want to do. You never really sell someone something, especially a house, that she does not want.

Checklists

Nothing takes the place of a good checklist outlining the tasks to be performed and the division of labor. Define at every possible juncture what is expected of everyone and most people will either comply with their appointed tasks or alter the checklist. Either way you are happy. A checklist of and for your own actions is a good example of a precise standard method of operation, a good defense, and a superb credibility builder.

Notes for Agency Selection

Company Form

If you are looking for a good place to implement a company form, I can think of no better area than that of buyer representation, especially regarding the clarification of the seller subagency system when the buyer is a customer. The courts are having a field day with brokers who are failing to inform the customer of the nature of the relationship that exists between buyer and broker.

Alternative Definition

Start by defining the alternatives, if there are any, and the expectations of the buyer that is a customer. Do this prior to any services being rendered so that everyone will have the same expectations of the extent of the services that are to be rendered. That way everyone will know when the agent has met those standards. Four objectives are at hand:

First, explain in advance either the extent of the options that are available or, in the event there are no options, the extent of the relationship between the buyer as a customer and the broker, salesperson, other agents and sellers. This must be done early, before the buyer starts to think of the agent as "my real estate person."

Second, if there are options available that include other relationships beyond the traditional seller subagency, explain the different types and the compensation alternatives, if any, which are intrinsic to each form offered by the company. This is in addition to any state-required or approved forms. The requirement imposed by the state to use their form is not necessarily for broker protection or as extensive a document as a cautious buyer's broker would require, but it does serve the state's purpose of informing the buyer of the relationship in some detail.

Third, and most important to the broker and salesperson, limit the apparent authority of the agent.

Fourth, describe the services that will be provided. Care needs to be taken here to describe not only what you will do, the extent of the service, but also those things for which you will not be responsible.

Agency Selection Form

The following indicates the extent of service, the agency relationship and compensation systems available from this company for prospective purchasers. Please review it in detail with our salesperson and select the form that best suits your needs. When accepted and signed by the broker, this will indicate the type of representation to be provided by Denver Canadian Realty, Inc. In the absence of any approved selection, the relationship will be such that we will act as subagents for various sellers, that is, as a traditional seller subagency.

Traditional Seller Agency

Under this relationship, we act as the agents for the various sellers who have listed their property with this office and as subagents for the listings that are available through other sellers' agents, either through the Multiple Listing Service or otherwise. We owe a fiduciary duty to those sellers and are compensated by receiving a part of the total commission payable to the seller's agent, the listing broker. This division of commissions varies between offices and sometimes between listings as each broker designates the amount of commission that that office is willing to pay to the successful subagent for locating a purchaser for the seller's property. There is no expense to you.

It is our professional pleasure and obligation to inform you, as a prospective purchaser, and as our customer, of many of the aspects affecting your decision to acquire real estate in this area. We will provide you with a list of the companies in this area that offer the following available services: title insurance, lending, property inspection services and the like. We will also direct you to the appropriate agencies to point out zoning and use requirements. Title companies offer different types of coverage and endorsements to accomplish various goals. We will help you become aware of the different options available so that you can make an informed selection.

We will provide you with information about the available lenders and a general brief description of the different types of loans that are available. There are, however, so many competing financing institutions, banks, savings and loan associations, credit unions, and mortgage companies in today's market, each having various options available, that many of the lenders know their ever-changing product lines better than anyone and are the best sources of the information. They like to assist you in the selection from their list of available products and arrange the loan best suited to your needs and requirements.

There is no substitution for a home inspection by a professional service, architect or engineer of your selection, if you feel it is necessary. We are not qualified, and, since we are not licensed engineers in this state, we are in fact prohibited from inspecting property and giving opinions as to a home's condition. We do not inspect nor warrant the physical condition of any property, regardless of whose agent we are. There are a variety of such inspection and home warranty services and engineers available ready to serve you in the inspection, certification, and insurance of the condition of the property.

We also verify, by obtaining a written statement from the city and county, the zoning and allowable use for the property and the status of the water and sewer supply. We can provide you with a map indicating the location of the school nearest to each property and the telephone number of that school so that you can inquire further if you so desire.

In short, we try to make every pertinent bit of information available to you so that you can make a good selection. The determination of the value of the property is something we cannot undertake. There are numerous appraisal services available, and the determination of value is often just a personal decision with a personal home. With the exposure you will have to the available properties and their asking prices, you should be able to arrive at a reasonable price determination. Often the price is determined by negotiation with the seller of the home you have selected and usually must also meet the requirements of the new first lender in order to obtain a new loan.

Please understand that we cannot be responsible for the extent of service or lack of service promised or delivered by any third party.

Buyer's Broker

Under either of the following options, we act as your agents and not as the agents or subagents for any seller. Before this type of agency can be selected, you need to realize that we already represent a number of sellers as their agents, their properties having already been listed with this company. It would be a conflict of interest for us to accept a Buyer's Broker Agreement if it is your intention to select one of these properties.

[This is an area of great concern. There seem to be no right answers when the buyer wants to see a seller's house that is listed with the broker. I have selected a tough stance to try to avoid liability. You will have to have a disclaimer in the listing agreement of every seller to deal with this alternative if you are going to accept agency for buyers. Seek legal counsel before using any information contained here. Read the alternative paragraphs with a little sense of humor and I think you will get an appreciation for the almost impossible dilemma of dual agency taken to the fullest extent.]

Should you determine that you are not interested in one of our listings and later decide that you are interested in such a listing, whether that listing existed at the time you employed us as your agents or subsequent to such employment, a full disclosure of this fact would have to be made to both you and the seller. In such an event, we would not be responsible or liable to you in any fashion whatsoever, as your agents or otherwise, and we would be obligated to reveal to the seller any information that we possessed that might assist the seller in making a determination of whether or not to sell his property to you.

Except for the foregoing situation, which is difficult for everyone, our capacity as your agents includes all the above services that we would ordinarily provide as seller's agents or subagents. In addition, we would also provide...[List the features that your company provides that are not part of the seller agency package.] Under this option, more fully described in the Exclusive Buyer Agency Contract, as required by the Real Estate Commission of the State of Colorado, you would be responsible for the payment of our fee. There are two options offered by this firm to meet that obligation.

After reviewing the foregoing alternatives, it is my understanding that you are acting as:

_____ Agent or subagent for various sellers.

_____ An agent for the buyer pursuant to the attached Exclusive Buyer Agency Contract.

Buyer: Dated: _____

_____   Broker:
                                Denver Canadian Realty, Inc.

_____   _____

                                by: Lee D. Weinstein, Broker

DENVER CANADIAN REALTY, INC.

Rejection of Subagency

I, the undersigned, as the authorized agent for the indicated broker, hereby reject the offer of subagency made through the vehicle of the Multiple Listing Service with regard to the following listed properties:

621 Pine Street
75 Manhattan Drive

From this point forward I will be acting as the agent for a buyer who wishes to remain undisclosed and will not be acting as the agent or subagent of either the seller or your firm.

It is our understanding that:

_____ I will be compensated by my client without contribution from either you or the seller.

_____ You will compensate me by paying me the sum of ___% of the final selling price, immediately upon the closing of any transaction involving one of my clients (buyers) purchasing either or both of the above properties.

_____ You will guarantee the payment by your seller of an amount equal to ___% of the listing price on the date of this communication, regardless of the ultimate selling price, payable upon the closing of any transaction wherein one of my buyers purchases any or all of the above properties.

Based on our understanding I am proceeding to show the indicated properties to my clients.

Denver Canadian Realty, Inc.

by: Lee D. Weinstein, Broker

Please indicate your acceptance of the terms herein by signing below:

Approved:

_____

DENVER CANADIAN
REALTY, INC.
420 Ponderosa Drive   Boulder, CO 80303
(303) 494-6661

Mr. William R. Listing-Broker
Seller's Realty and Insurance
23 West Coop Lane
Commission City, WA 80000

  Re: No. 7 Benthaven Way

Dear Bill:

  Thank you for taking the time to talk with me on Monday March 2, 1987, about the above property. As I indicated to you then, our initial contact, I am rejecting your kind offer of subagency with regard to this property. In this particular instance I am operating as a buyer's broker or for my own account and do not want to have any fiduciary duty to either you or the seller.

  I was happy that you did not take such an announcement too seriously and were still able to confide in me the secrets that the seller had confided in you. The indication that the seller would take a lesser price will be very advantageous in my representation of the purchaser and will probably speed a fast sale.

  It was our understanding that, regardless of my agency capacity, you will pay my brokerage firm, Denver Canadian Realty, Inc., a co-op commission equal to the commission that you have indicated in the MLS book as being available for subagents and that you will pay such immediately upon the closing of the transaction. You understand that the financial arrangements that I have made with my principal cannot be disclosed since I take my fiduciary duties very seriously.

  Thank you for arranging the showing on the 4th of March. I will expect a constant flow of confidential information and will do everything that I can to assist you in taking advantage of your client, the seller. It is always a pleasure to work with you in a real estate transaction.

  If the information contained in this letter does not match your understanding, respond immediately by messenger as I am operating on the assumption that this accurately reflects our agreement.

      Sincerely,
      Denver Canadian Realty, Inc.

      James C. Smittkamp

      by: James C. "Jim" Smittkamp
      Authorized Sales Agent

Rules of the Road for the Buyer

Mr. and Mrs. Jonathan A. Goodman
Apartment 610 A
12th and Main Street
Denver, CO 80303

    Re: Services for Purchasers

Dear Mr. and Mrs. Goodman:

    Let me be the first to welcome you to Denver, Colorado, and to our office. We have a small professional cadre of agents and support staff that have been doing business at this location for fourteen months. Satisfied clients and customers are our primary concern.

    Each state has its own laws, rules, and regulations concerning real estate in general and real estate, salespersons, brokers, lenders, title companies and the like in specific. I sometimes wonder how so many different systems could evolve. In Colorado, the state licenses a broker for each office, and all contracts or agreements that bind the company must be signed by the broker to be effective. I am happy to work for Lee D. Weinstein, the licensed broker for Denver Canadian Realty, Inc.

    Our company acts as agents for, and represents, many owners that have listed their properties with us for sale. It is our hope that you can find a nice home that will fit your needs, within your budget, from our inventory of available properties.

    In addition, as members of the Multiple Listing Service, we have access to and can show you literally hundreds of additional properties encompassing all the properties listed by other member brokers. We cooperate with other brokerage offices as subagents of their sellers. As one of the licensed agents for Denver Canadian Realty, Inc., I work hard to assist buyers with their real estate needs, and I am sure that I will be able to provide you with the information you request concerning almost all of the aspects of the local real estate market, including sources of available financing, so that you will be able to make an informed selection of a new home.

We are proud to adhere to the Department of Housing and Urban Development's Fair Housing Standards and the Constitutions of both the United States and Colorado. We want you to realize that you are free to, and in fact we encourage you to, make an offer on any house that you select. The only factors limiting your selection are the same ones that limit everyone: the amount of money you have available to spend for a down payment, the amount that you can or will borrow, and the size of the monthly payments that you desire.

Neighborhood mix or makeup are impossible for us to determine. This is a totally open market with equal access to everyone. I am sure that you will be able to select a home that meets your needs from a wide variety of available homes either listed with our firm or through the Muliple Listing Service.

We are happy to show you and your family as many homes as you desire in any part of the city and surrounding county and provide you with the information at our disposal to aid you in determining the right new home for you to acquire. The different available locations vary from the urban city-center to the rural country locations. Only you can decide which home is located in the area you desire, is best suited to your physical needs, and meets the financial requirements you determine are within your budget.

In this state, there are a few different options available to buyers for the acquisition of our services. A detailed explanation of the extent of and cost attributable to each option is on the reverse of the Agency Selection Form. Please review the available options and select the option that you feel best suits your needs. Indicate your selection on the Agency Selection Form and return it to our office. I will obtain the broker's signature and give you a copy for your records. Absent any selection to the contrary, we will act as sellers' subagents.

If you are ever unable to reach me or just want to talk to the broker for this company, please feel free to contact Lee Weinstein either in the office, 494-3000, or at his home, 494-4664. Lee is a well-respected broker and I am proud to work for him. I am sure that he and I will be able to assist you in your selection of a new home in this area.

Most sincerely,
Denver Canadian Realty, Inc.

Peter A. Walters

by: Peter A. Walters, Salesperson

cc: Lee D. Weinstein, Broker

Seller is also a Buyer

It is perceived as the best of all worlds when the seller, having listed his property with the broker, through the salesperson, now also wants to purchase a new or additional piece of property. The agent and the seller already have established a rapport and are able to speak with candor. The agent has learned not only the likes and dislikes of his client but also the secrets of his client, the amount of money available, the relative financial worth of the various entities that his client may use to acquire property, the extent to which the client will go to attain his goals, and the overall strategy of the client.

Often forgotten is the fact that the client is now a customer. Most buyers feel that the agent with whom they are working is their agent. A recent survey indicated that that was the case for seventy-one percent of those questioned. Imagine what the client feels after he has listed with the broker or agent and is now going out to search for new acquisitions. I would guess that nearly one hundred percent of all sellers that are seeking to purchase real estate with their listing agents are convinced that the agent is working for them. If they ever knew the distinction between agent, subagent, and buyer's broker, that distinction is probably lost when the client becomes a buyer.

Absent an indication to the contrary, there is no doubt that the ultimate dual agency arrangement has been created. Although I dislike the use of dual agency, this has to be the definition of the term.

The agent becomes the subagent for the new seller, unless he specifies to the new seller's agents that he is functioning in this instance as a buyer's broker. Most people do not do this. They do not discuss the new relationship with their principal, and they fail further to get any agreement about compensation. So, in fact, they are subagents of various sellers. What is more, such a person may still be considered by the former seller-client, now buyer-customer, as that former client's agent. Confusing? Think about how a court or an uninitiated individual might see it. There has been no indication that the agency relationship has changed, and, therefore, the seller-turned-buyer has no reason to feel that the former agent is no longer an agent. Finally, the agents for the various new sellers whose homes you are going to show, do not know of your dual capacity and therefore may provide you with information under the mistaken assumption that you are their subagents.

All this would probably go unnoticed except for the fact that the agent knows the indicated information about the buyer which he is obligated to disclose to his principal, the listing broker for the property proposed for acquisition. This does not occur, and, therefore, the agent is liable to both the seller and the buyer. There is no defense. The only saving grace is that most listing agents do not rely upon nor trust their subagents and so are not injured by the lack of information. The rub comes when the seller discovers a problem and starts to look for a deep pocket. The listing broker, being liable for the actions and inactions of the subagent, misguided or not, is now open for a lose-lose lawsuit.

The different states have a variety of different laws and interpretations of their laws that can leave the broker and agent in doubt as to the availability of the buyer's broker alternative. Do not be led into a false sense of security if you practice real estate in a state that has laws which seem to indicate that a buyer's brokerage is not proper, and, therefore, everyone is a seller's agent. The courts in these states, in an effort to protect a purchaser or obtain a desired result, could easily assume the existence of a duty similar to that of an agent and impose that duty upon the unsuspecting former seller's agent. No matter what the arrangement, clarify it with the seller-turned-buyer and, if different for the assumed subagency, further clarify it with the other seller's agents that you contact.

The following letter offers a lot of alternative paragraphs depending upon your policy of offering buyer agency or not. In the event that you do offer buyers' brokerage services, you may not want to use all of the indicated forms of payment arrangements, or may have others of your own. This is not an endorsement of the buyers' broker movement. It is just a place to start in defining your relationship with your former seller-client to protect you in your future dealings.

I have chosen the Colorado Real Estate Commission-approved forms to use as examples. The alternative paragraphs may be used in Colorado, since the approved forms are not the only disclosres that are permissable in Colorado, as well as in other states.

Seller is also a Buyer

DENVER CANADIAN
REALTY, INC.
420 Ponderosa Drive   Boulder, CO 80303
(303) 494-6661

Mr. and Mrs. Gary S. Joiner
4750 Table Mesa Drive
Boulder, CO 80303

Re: 75 McCoy Drive, Windhaven

Dear Mr. and Mrs. Joiner:

Jim has told me that you have selected him to assist you on behalf of this office in the selection of your new home. No one is more qualified than Jim, since he has not only had the opportunity to get to know you and to determine what you desire in your new home, but he is also very familiar with many of the properties available in this area. As members of the Multiple Listing Service, we have access not only to our inventory of listings but also to numerous properties available in this area that have been listed by the other brokers who are also members.

Unless you indicate otherwise, Jim will assist you as a subagent for the various sellers offering their homes for sale, either through this office or other sellers' agents in other offices, and not as your agent. To be sure that you are aware of the various relationships that are offered to our customers, I have briefly outlined the major alternative agency relationships that [this office undertakes] [are available in the marketplace]. [Although discussed briefly below for your information, please understand that this office does not act as a buyer's broker. We feel that our extensive inventory of listings makes us a strong office for the sale of property for numerous sellers. We do this job very well and are happy to assist, although not represent, buyers in their search for a new home. If we also started to accept buyers as principals, we would have continuous conflicts of interest, especially when our buyers wanted to see property listed by us as sellers' agents. For this reason, we accept single agency only, and represent sellers as agents or subagents. Over the years, this has always been our company's position, and we have helped numerous buyers select from our listings and those of other brokers.]

Buyer's Broker

If you wish, [although this is not the prevalent agency arrangement followed by this firm,] we can accept employment as your agent, that is, as a buyer's broker, to assist you in the selection of a new home. This would be a similar relationship to the agency relationship we enjoy as the agents for the sale of your home. A few words about the various relationships follow:

Many of the agents for various other sellers offer to split the commission that they receive from their sellers and cooperate with other brokers on a basis that is determined in advance as a result of negotiation between brokers. There is no standard split. This offer is made to prospective subagents only and generally not to a prospective buyer's broker. Our Buyer's Broker Agreement, which incorporates the Exclusive Buyer Agency Contract approved and mandated by the State of Colorado, contains all the terms of this arrangement. It must be completed and signed by me on behalf of Denver Canadian Realty, Inc., as well as by Jim Smittkamp prior to our becoming your agent for the purchase of any real estate. The agreement specifies the alternative methods available for your payment for our services as your agent for the acquisition of real estate.

There are three different methods for our compensation as a buyer's broker offered by this firm. They vary somewhat and have differing effects on our relationship with other sellers' agents.

Direct Compensation

You agree to pay us a commission directly and in full upon the completion of our tasks as outlined in the Buyer's Broker Agreement. In such a case, we will indicate each time we contact other sellers' brokers, and also so indicate on all offers submitted to other sellers' brokers, that you are paying us directly and in full. Also, if you so desire, although we discourage it, we will state the amount or percentage of such compensation. It is our hope that such a disclosure will allow the seller to reduce the commission which the seller would normally be obligated to pay to his agent and, therefore, accept a lower price, decreased by an amount approximately equal to the amount of the foregone co-op commission. This does not always work because it requires the seller's broker to voluntarily renegotiate his commission schedule with the seller, something some sellers' brokers are reluctant to consent to.

Limited Seller Contribution

We will attempt to induce the various sellers' agents to split their commission with our firm, as if we were their agent, that is, subagents of their seller.

If successful, to the extent that we are actually compensated by the seller's agent, we will reduce your commission obligation to us, as indicated in the Buyer's Broker Agreement. This reduction will equal the amount of compensation we actually receive from the seller's agent. If, after the application of the amount received from the seller's agent, there remains a balance outstanding, it will be your obligation. Sometimes this is successful. This arrangement and the amounts involved are indicated prior to any showings and again in the contract. We cannot be responsible for the failure of the seller or his agent to perform as they indicate they will. As with the first option, this requires the consent and cooperation of the other seller's broker.

Total Seller Compensation

The last and least-likely-to-succeed option provides that the seller's broker will cooperate with this office as if we were his subagent. That broker would then pay us a fee equal to what would have been the normal cooperative split determined between our two offices or negotiated for this particular transaction. This is the system adopted by our firm because we feel that it encourages all possible assistance by all brokers, regardless of affiliation. However, it also requires the other listing brokers to do something that they are not always obligated to do.

There is no set or agreed-upon practice for the division—or split—of the listing broker's commission, nor will there ever be one. Each real estate office, whether a member of the board or not, is free to, and in fact does, negotiate commission splits with the other brokerage offices on terms acceptable to each set of brokers. Neither the board nor the state is interested in delving into or establishing standards for commission divisions because these are the separate business practices established by each office. In all instances where we are acting as your agents and not as the subagents of the seller, without regard to the source of compensation, we disclose both the fact that we are your agents and the manner of our compensation. We do this on our initial contact with the agents of other sellers and again in the contract so that everyone knows whom we are representing. You should review the information attached to the Buyer's Broker Agreement in detail in order to understand what services we provide in our capacity as sellers' subagents versus those that are provided as your agent for the selection of real estate. In either event, we are always interested in your concerns and in providing you with all the available facts and information so that you can make your selection intelligently.

Seller's Subagent

The most generally utilized relationship finds us acting as subagents for various sellers as we help you gain access to and view properties that you feel might fit your needs but which are listed by our competitors. This subagency relationship includes providing you with information and sources of information to make your decision-making as easy as possible and gives you our knowledge of the available lenders, title companies, inspection experts and other professionals to help you with the decisions about the and financing of your new home. We are not your agent. You do not have any obligation to compensate us since we are paid by the other seller's agent through a cooperative split of the total commission paid to the other broker. In this case, in Colorado, Commission Rule E-35 requires that we tell you before we start to assist you as a buyer with any real estate needs that we are the subagent for various sellers. The law also requires that we give you the following oral disclosure. The Commission, although they do not mandate it, has encouraged this disclosure to be written. We agree and that is why we have included it in this letter.

<u>NOTICE TO PROSPECTIVE REAL ESTATE PURCHASER</u>

Commission-Approved Form (Colorado)

Lee D. Weinstein, (broker) Denver Canadian Realty, Inc., and I, James C. Smittkamp, and all other agents of the broker are or will be acting as agents of the seller with the duty to represent the seller's interests and will not be your agent.

Author's Plain Language Version

Lee D. Weinstein, James C. Smittkamp, and Denver Canadian Realty, Inc., and all other real estate agents are acting as agents for, and therefore owe a fiduciary duty to, the seller in this transaction. We are not acting as your agents.

Author's Additional Buyer Brokerage Language

If you desire to employ us to act as your agents, provided we are not already engaged by the seller of any property that you may be interested in, you will have to do so with a separate written agreement. This agreement must be executed by you and by my broker before we begin showing you any property.

In addition, you will probably see one of the following clauses inserted in purchase contracts:

CONTRACT-DISCLOSURE REAFFIRMATION

Commission-Approved Form (Colorado)

Purchaser hereby acknowledges prior, timely receipt of notice that Lee D. Weinstein (broker), Denver Canadian Realty, Inc., and its agents are agents of seller and are not representing purchaser as purchaser's agent in this transaction.

Author's Alternate Version

Purchaser acknowledges that, prior to talking about purchaser's needs or any specific property, broker (Denver Canadian Realty, Inc., Lee D. Weinstein, and James C. Smittkamp) indicated that broker was not acting as purchaser's agent and was not representing the purchaser in this transaction. Broker indicated to purchaser that, should purchaser desire to employ broker to act as purchaser's agent, purchaser would have had to have done so by a separate written agreement. This agreement would have had to have been executed by purchaser and broker before broker could begin showing purchaser any property and providing broker was not already engaged by the seller of any property which purchaser might be interested in.

Memorandum of Previous Oral Disclosure

This is a memorandum of our previous oral understanding, made prior to discussing this or any other property with you as purchaser, that James C. Smittkamp, Denver Canadian Realty, Inc., and the broker, Lee D. Weinstein are acting as agents for the seller of this property and the sellers of all other property that we may show or present to you. We are not and will not act as your agents unless you enter into a separate written agreement indicating that we are your agents and then only under the provision that we are not already agents for any particular seller.

Thank you for taking the time to review this lengthy letter. Unless you and I, on behalf of Denver Canadian Realty, Inc., execute a Buyer's Broker

Agreement, we will be acting as subagents for the various other sellers that own the property you wish to view and purchase and not as your agents. Please let either of us know if there is anything that we can do to facilitate showing you property and providing you with the information you require to make your selection.

Most sincerely,
Denver Canadian Realty, Inc.

Lee D. Weinstein

by: Lee D. Weinstein, Broker

The Use of Professionals

Delegation

There is no need to be all things to all people. If there is someone else who can preform the required task, their services need to be recommended and encouraged. Should the buyer be reluctant, a cover letter is a nice way to indicate the importance of your suggestion. I often say, "You realize that I have got to give you a letter indicating that I thought you should seek an independent appraisal or a structural inspection prior to signing the contract." By this time they are ready for that statement. Follow it up with a letter.

The Referral

The agent exposes herself to great danger with the consistent recommendation of a friend or associate. You will not only look bad if there is ever a problem, but you may have put yourself in a lose-lose position. If you are going to recommend the services of a professional, mentioning that other clients have seemed satisfied or have told you that they were pleased with the service might be a tactful way to indicate that one person is in fact better than the other. Offer a list of at least three separate individuals compiled from your known resources, the yellow pages, a circular put out by the certifying organization, or a professional publication.

Referrals are a good way to lose a customer and rarely make any money. Agents live with a referral long after the transaction is closed and the money spent.

Complexity

The status of the modern real estate transaction today simply does not lend itself to the general broker who is an expert in everything. The buyer will buy without your having to obligate yourself. Let the buyer decide on the expert and employ the expert personally. Do not arrange for or contract for the expert.

Opinions

Too often agents give title insurance opinions, saying something like, "Sure the title is OK. Those are just standard exceptions." You might hear a new agent or an agent helping a good friend say, "This is the best loan available," or "Tom Richmond at Richmond Mortgage is the best; whatever he says is what you should do," feeling compelled to have an opinion or the need to "keep the deal together."

Inflation is gone. Neither you nor a buyer can simply sell a mistake. The parties are going to rely on your statements, and, should they prove to be in error, you will be responsible and so will the broker. The use of standard letters can help clear the air and explain in specific detail the duties you have and have not assumed. This will help to limit the liability of everyone, including your broker. Stay out of the glib opinion business and just offer responsible service.

Drafting Tip

Note that the next letter indicates not that there is a contract between the parties but just that the seller signed the offer before a certain date and time. The conclusion to be drawn by the *buyer* is that there is a contract.

Mr. and Mrs. Jonathan A. Goodman
Apartment 610 A
12th and Main Street
Denver, CO 80303

Re: 909 First Street

Dear Mr. and Mrs. Goodman:

Congratulations on your decision to make an offer on the property at 909 First Street. [I love to be the bearer of good news. Your contract was signed by the seller last night, January 5th, at 4:30 P.M.] I am pleased that you were able to locate a home you feel is affordable and that you think you will enjoy. There are several items that you have elected to include in your offer that you will need to address to your satisfaction in order to insure that the transaction is completed as you desire and that your new home meets all your requirements.

As you know, our firm is comprised of professional real estate people whose job it is to represent sellers in assisting buyers [or act as buyers' brokers assisting buyers] in locating houses which they feel are suited to their needs and which they feel financially qualified to purchase. Once that is done, we encourage the selection and use of the services of other professionals to satisfy the requirements indicated in the contract. Your satisfaction is important, and you will certainly want to avail yourself of the assurances you desire. We are not in the lending, title insurance, termite inspection, structural inspection, radon testing or home warranty businesses; nor are we in the business of providing legal or accounting services. Being real estate agents is a full time job in itself.

Although we all have received recommendations from previous clients and customers regarding their selections and favorites and have a list of our own friends, we cannot recommend any one firm or person who we think will fill your needs. That selection is a personal one left up to you. To provide you with a place to start, however, I have attached a list of people who have been utilized by other buyers in the past or who have done work for us. You understand that we cannot accept responsibility for the work product of any of these firms or individuals. The decision to utilize one or more of the following firms or individuals or not is your personal decision. This is not a complete list, nor is the inclusion or exclusion of any particular professional a tribute, endorsement or criticism.

We hope the list is helpful in making your choice. If I can be of any further assistance, please do not hesitate to let me know.

Most sincerely,
Denver Canadian Realty, Inc.

James C. Smittkamp

by: Jim Smittkamp, Salesperson

cc: Suzanne Wilson, Broker
Enc.: List

DENVER CANADIAN
REALTY, INC.
420 Ponderosa Drive   Boulder, CO 80303
(303) 494-6661

Mr. and Mrs. Jonathan A. Goodman
Apartment 610 A
12th and Main Street
Denver, CO 80303

    Re: 909 First Street

Dear Jon and Mimi:

    Congratulations on your decision to make an offer to purchase this particular property. I am pleased that you were able to locate an older home you feel is affordable and that you think you will enjoy. As you know, with all older homes, there are a number of areas that may require special attention. We recommend that, in addition to obtaining the normal radon gas, septic system and water quality tests you requested, you also consult a structural engineer and a termite inspector. These are terms you included in the contract, and you will need to get started as soon as possible after the offer is accepted since there is often a delay between the time a test is requested and the time the results are obtained. I want to try to stay within the dates outlined in your contract so that there is no chance that you will lose the property. In addition, your prompt attention will allow us to indicate to our sellers the status of the contract so that they can make decisions on other proposals, which they may elect to accept as alternative contracts if and when they arrive.

    The contract indicates that you must give written notice of any dissatisfaction [directly to the seller, with a copy delivered] to us as the seller's agents prior to noon on Wednesday the 12th or the condition, #19(3), requiring a satisfactory inspection will be deemed to have been satisfied.

    Our firm is comprised of professional real estate people who are familiar with properties in this area. Please know that we are not soils engineers or structural engineers and, therefore, cannot be responsible for the physical condition of the property or the soil it rests upon. The services of other professionals are required to satisfy these questions in your mind as well as the other requirements indicated in the contract and to provide you with the assurances you desire. Transactions today are complex and require the talents of lending institutions, title insurance companies, termite inspectors, radon testers, and sometimes home warranty underwriters, not to mention the services of a lawyer or accountant.

We encourage you to seek and select the counsel of the experts of your choice in order to insure that you are satisfied with all of the complex aspects of the purchase of your new home. Please understand that we cannot accept responsibility for the work product of any of these firms or individuals. I too must rely on professionals when I acquire real property because the talents they possess are just not within my area of expertise. If I can be of any further assistance please do not hesitate to let me know.

Most sincerely,
Denver Canadian Realty, Inc.

James C. Smittkamp

by: Jim Smittkamp, Sales Agent

cc: Suzanne Wilson, Broker

Sales Contract Clauses

Although this is not a forms manual for completing a sales contract, it seems like a logical place to include a few ideas for clauses that pertain to the items discussed in this book. Try not only to determine the conditions that must be met, the dates and often the times within which these conditions must be satisfied, but also the default in the event no action is taken. As a seller's agent, I would think that the default would indicate removal of or elimination of the condition if action were not taken by the buyer. Before you get carried away, remember that in almost all circumstances, if the buyer defaults, the seller will not compel performance and will be relegated to retain the vast sum of money pledged as earnest money. The seller will only obtain that after some hassle. Although there is no substitute for a well-drafted contract, it is money and the fear of its loss that motivates the average person. Try to collect a sum that represents a significant amount of money for both the buyer and seller. These clauses are more extensive than you may require for the average transaction. I have attempted to give you one master rather than ten for a particular series of problems.

Professionals

Purchaser is advised to seek, select and retain the professionals she desires to investigate the following: the presence and extent of radon gas or other hazardous materials or substances; the physical condition of the property, including the structural integrity; the condition of appliances, heating, plumbing, air conditioning, electrical and other mechanical and structural devices and systems; the condition of the soils and surrounding soils; the existence of, proximity to, adequacy and expense of utilizing or obtaining the services for water, sewer, natural gas, electrical, television and other services and utilities; the terms and conditions of all covenants and restrictions that affect the property; the condition and extent of the title and rights, duties and obligations that may exist as a result of documents existing of record and that may arise as a result of the obligations, duties, rights and privileges this transaction may impose or create, including the terms conditions and provisions of financing arrangements; and the character of allowed uses, zoning or other public or private regulations, codes, ordinances or the like that may effect the property.

This is a contract which contemplates the purchase and sale of real property. All parties are hereby advised and have been advised to seek competent legal, accounting and such other advice as they in their own discretion determine to be advisable. The broker and all agents and subagents are not and have not offered any legal, tax or accounting advice with regard to this or any other transaction involving these parties or otherwise.

Agent's Disclaimer

Neither the seller, the listing or selling broker, nor any of their agents or employees are responsible for the condition of the property, the representations of the seller, as outlined on the Property Disclosure Sheet—attached hereto as Exhibit P—or for other representations made directly to the buyer, or for the items outlined in the foregoing paragraph.

Purchaser acknowledges that, prior to completing this offer, he has received a copy of the Property Condition Report [Soils Report] completed by the seller which describes the condition of the property.

Neither the seller, the buyer, nor any of their agents are relying on any representation or omission of or by any real estate agent associated with this transaction for any decision as to the value of the property, the condition of the property, the decision to purchase the property, or the terms and conditions of sale that are incorporated in this contract.

The parties acknowledge that none of the brokers or agents associated with this transaction has made an inspection of the property and none is responsible for any defect that such an inspection might have revealed.

Aspects of the Property

The purchase price indicated was determined by me after making a careful inspection of the property. I have not relied upon any information printed in the Multiple Listing Service or on any listing information sheets as I understand that they are for the use of broker members only and may contain errors, such as the total amount of square footage, the size of the lot, the school district, the availability of water, etc. I have relied upon the Listing Addendum, completed by the seller and delivered to me before I made this offer. My conclusions are based on information that I have obtained and verified to my satisfaction without relying upon statements made by any agent of the seller.

HOW Warranty Status

I understand that there is a HOW warranty currently covering the property. I have made an independent investigation as to the term remaining, the extent of coverage, and the extent to which the available coverage has been utilized. I realize that the broker is not warranting the condition of the property and is not responsible for physical defects that might come to light after the sale.

AS IS

I am purchasing the property in AS IS condition without any warranty from the seller or any agent of the seller, including, but not limited to the agent indicated in this contract, that the property is fit for any particular purpose. I understand and have been encouraged to have the property inspected by experts of my selection. I realize that the broker is not an engineer and is not warranting the structural condition of the property nor the condition of any appliances or systems, or otherwise.

Entire Deal

This contract incorporates all of the terms and conditions of all agreements between the parties, the buyer and seller. There are no promises, agreements, or representations, except as outlined herein. Except as expressly stated in this contract, neither the broker nor the sales agent has made any promises to induce any party to enter into this contract.

Buyer's Agency Fee Clause (Short Form)

The indicated agent, Denver Canadian Realty, Inc., through its broker and agents ("DCR") is not acting as agent or subagent of the seller. DCR is the agent of the buyer. DCR owes no fiduciary duty to the seller or to the seller's agents. Seller hereby agrees to pay DCR, as consideration for DCR's securing the buyer in this transaction, at the time of the closing of the transaction a sum equal to ___% of the gross selling price. This shall be DCR's sole compensation.

Buyer's Agency Fee Clause (Another Form)

As previously indicated to the (seller) listing brokerage company, the indicated agent, Denver Canadian Realty, Inc., through its broker and agents ("DCR") is not acting as agent or subagent of the seller. DCR is the agent of the buyer. DCR owes no fiduciary duty to the seller or to the seller's agents. Seller hereby agrees to pay DCR, as consideration for DCR's securing the buyer in this transaction, and hereby instructs his broker to pay DCR, at the time of the closing of the transaction a sum equal to ___% of the gross selling price. This shall be DCR's sole compensation. Purchaser's obligation to purchase the subject property is specifically conditional upon timely payment of the indicated commission.

Multiple sources of payment for a single broker, in this case a buyer's broker, are a problem we need to address. Colorado seems to be following the general rule by limiting the the buyer's broker to one source of compensation, absent written disclosure and agreement to the contrary. The following is Colorado's Rule E-33 dealing with this issue:

"When a licensee represents a purchaser or lessee of real property pursuant to any agency contract, he shall not accept compensation from the owner or owner's agent unless written disclosure of the agency relationship with the purchaser or lessee is made and express written consent given by all parties to the transaction."

DENVER CANADIAN
REALTY, INC.
420 Ponderosa Drive   Boulder, CO 80303
(303) 494-6661

Mr. and Mrs. Jonathan A. Goodman
c/o Martha Douglas
Douglas and Company Real Estate
12th and Main Street
Denver, CO 80303

    Re: 909 First Street

Dear Mr and Mrs. Goodman:

    In response to your inquiry about the extent of the Home Owners Warranty (HOW) on the property, I contacted Janine Lombardi at 696-3000 and she indicated that there was a policy, #34-098-NA-069, currently in effect. I would suggest that you talk with Janine directly so that she can answer your questions. That way there will be nothing lost in the translation and you can ask follow-up questions without having to contact me.

    Since our firm has a policy that prohibits us from making any guarantees with regard to any property, I always encourage interested buyers to talk directly with the insurance agency to avoid confusion. I would encourage you to inquire about the extent of the coverage, the term remaining, the balance of the unexpired limits which remains available. Thank you for your understanding. If you reach an impasse with HOW, please do not hesitate to let me know and I will try to find the person over there who can assist you.

                Sincerely,
                Denver Canadian Realty, Inc.

                by: Jim Smittkamp, Sales Agent

cc: Lee D. Weinstein, Broker
    Oliver E. Frascona

Chapter Four
Financing Alternatives

Assumption, Subject To, and Novation

More than any other aspect of a transaction, except possibly an undetectable defect in the condition of the property which was not discoverable and which does not show its ugly head until well after the closing, financing has become the hotbed of potential liability and loss. Much like latent defects, problems with financing can exist in a dormant state well into the future. The advent of complex arrangements and extensive television coverage of what some might consider "creative" methods of acquisition and financing that are not normally utilized has partially educated the public and left them often worse off than before the process began. The misconceptions about financing that prevail among all segments of society and even in the ranks of attorneys and some real estate professionals never cease to amaze me.

The disclosure and explanation of the seller's involvement in the financing is best given at the time the listing contract is completed, but it may also be appropriate to give it again at the time of the presentation of a contract. In any event, before the seller signs a contract that indicates one of these three alternate forms of seller involvement in the existing financing, a disclosure must be made.

The differences that arise from a transfer of property that (1) is subject to the existing financing, or (2) allows the assumption of the existing loan, or (3) requires a novation, are becoming the nightmares of the 1980s and probably will continue into the 1990s for the broker. In addition, any of the foregoing alternatives can be coupled with a seller carry-back or owner-carry second mortgage, just to keep the field more complex.

Financing that is assumable may be the factor that induces a buyer to purchase a particular house, yet the agent often fails to adequately explain the ramifications of the different alternatives until after the sale has been agreed upon or even after closing.

Although this is not an exhaustive presentation, the general differences between the alternatives follow.

Assumption

"The promise to pay the debt of another" is the definition of an assumption. You will note that the definition makes no mention of consent being sought nor obtained by the lender. That issue is addressed later. Assumption agreements are two-party agreements between the person who is going to accept responsibility for the payment of the obligation and the individual to whom the promise is made. The recipient of the promise may or may not already have an obligation to discharge the debt. An example of the latter might be an astute broker who previously accepted the property as part of a guaranteed sale and wisely took the property subject to the loan and, therefore, is not personally obligated to repay the loan. The broker may, nevertheless, whether as a result of a prior promise, or just in an effort to protect the prior borrowers, or simply to make sure there are as many defendants as possible if the transaction should go into default, require the new purchaser to assume the obligation.

Assumption imposes a personal obligation and liability upon the individual making the promise to repay the debt according to its terms. It is important to note, however, that there is no mention of a release of liability for the prior obligor, or borrower. A common misconception, even among some attorneys, is that an assumption releases the original obligor, usually the seller, from any ongoing personal obligation to repay the debt. The easy rule to remember is that no one is released from any obligation to pay unless the lender does so in writing. Therefore, the assumption of a debt merely adds another obligor for the lender to pursue. In some states, there are laws that prohibit some lenders from obtaining personal deficiency judgments against borrowers, and, therefore, this effect of an assumption is reduced.

Subject To

The key distinction in a "subject to" transaction is the lack of any personal obligation on the part of the buyer to retire the obligation, that is, it entails no personal liability. In either event, the property is transferred with the existing loan intact. In this instance, the buyer pays the lender because if he or she does not, the lender will foreclose on the property and the buyer's equity will probably be lost. The larger the down payment, the less the risk to the seller of eventual foreclosure because the buyer will have a lot to lose. A broker, doing a guaranteed sale would want to take property subject to the existing financing so that he will not be personally liable for repayment indefinitely. Such a broker, in addition to disclosing to his client the seller that he would not be obligated on the loan and thus not responsible for its ultimate repayment, would want to insure that his transferee assumed the loan.

Novation

Novation is often confused and merged in some people's minds with the idea of an "approved" assumption. Be careful. The lender, when it accepts the new purchaser and qualifies that purchaser for the assumption, may grant a release of the old borrower. Then a novation will have occurred. The lender may, however, retain all parties on the debt. A common misconception is that an assumption with a change in the rate or other terms becomes a novation and the old seller, borrower, is automatically released. This used to be a safe assumption—no pun intended—but many new loan agreements state otherwise. A written clarification of everyone's rights, duties, and obligations after an approved assumption is very important.

Case in Point

The sellers, one of whom was a tax attorney and the other a chemical engineer, filed a complaint with a real estate licensing board requesting that the board revoke the license of a broker who failed to explain the difference between an assumption and a novation prior to listing the property and prior to the contract for sale being executed. The attorney for the broker argued that the difference was surely in the knowledge bank of the tax attorney. The attorney general, representing the state, replied that "Just being an attorney, even a tax attorney who did not deal with real estate on a regular basis, was not enough to let the broker off the hook for not explaining the difference."

This occurred at a hearing to determine if the broker and salesman should have their licenses revoked. A very serious hearing.

Free Living

As a result of the slow economic conditions existing in some areas that have not experienced the rapid inflationary expansion prevalent in recent years, plus the time-consuming and previously obscure foreclosure laws, the rules preventing or delaying the entry of deficiency judgments in some states, and the delay imposed as a result of the modern Bankruptcy Code, some owners are realizing that they can stop making payments on the existing loan, whether they assumed it or took the property subject to the loan, and live in the residence for from six to eighteen months rent free. The longest I know of is forty-two months—that's right, forty-two months—without the owner making a single payment. That case, in which I was a participant, involved an FHA loan that was resold during the period of default three times and nobody knew what was going on.

A family with an income can amass a good deal of money in that time period and, therefore, have the down payment for the next home when they are finally removed form their current residence. You got it. This person then has the cash to assume another non-qualifying assumption (VA, FHA, subject to some restrictions and some private and conventional financing) and could be looking at your current listing. Buyers with that kind of cash are rarely the subject of scrutiny, almost never trigger the request for a credit report, are hard to recognize, and even harder for some brokers and sellers and other desperate people to turn down.

Price and Loan Adjustments

Discount points and loan origination fees also need complete, timely, and adequate presentation prior to the seller or buyer becoming obligated to a contract. Does the seller have to pay the agreed-upon discount even if the buyer uses the money to obtain a lower interest rate? Is a discount point different from a loan origination fee? The payment of large sums to induce a lender to make a loan is being viewed by some regulators as a reduction in the effective purchase price and, therefore, a reduction of the amount upon which the commission is calculated. The use of zero coupon bonds, gems, questionable paper to offset the purchase price is receiving close scrutiny. Sometimes it can be very embarrassing when the broker cannot explain the ramifications of using such items.

Case in Point

A broker provides in the contract, at the direction and suggestion of the purchaser, that a seller, in order to obtain the listed price, which both purchaser and seller have verbally agreed is in excess of the fair market value of the property, accept as part payment of the listed price a zero coupon bond. The bond had a current market value of about $2,000 and a future value, upon redemption in twenty years, of about $12,000. The seller is then to give the purchaser a credit equal to the future value of the bond. The seller, an astute older woman, not only agrees to the proposal but counters lower, thus increasing the amount of the future value of the bond and also thereby changing the current value and cost of the bond that will be acquired.

The transaction closes pursuant to the terms of the contract and the bond is purchased and delivered to the seller. The seller, now out of state and looking for a method to extract funds from the broker, files a complaint with the Real Estate Commission. They determine that there should have been no commission charged on the amount of the purchase price represented by the future value of the bond and "suggest" that the broker make an appropriate refund.

How lucky the broker was. In this particular case he did nothing wrong. However, with a little change in circumstances, he could have had a securities problem. He could have had a problem with a side agreement that was not available to the new lender who made the new loan. He could have gone to jail. Do not worry, he is still out there waiting to be your subagent.

The perils of suggesting, drafting, structuring, or even allowing, as one regulator expressed it, a seller to accept some form of creative financing deserve a similar detailed explanation and disclosure prior to placing such terms in a listing agreement or sales contract. Whenever the seller is going to remain involved with the financing of the real estate, that seller is going to have a tendency to look to the broker to "guarantee" the performance of the buyer.

A more in-depth review of seller financing is only a few pages ahead.

Transfers Without Prior Lender Consent, Silent Assumptions

With rates being as low as they have been lately, this form of financing is less prevalent than it was a few years ago. Still, many people decide to run the risk of a transfer without the prior consent of the lender, sometimes known as a "silent assumption." With the advent of new FHA rules, this may become a more prevalent situation if notification of FHA is not desired by one or both of the parties. Such an assumption requires as a minimum an absolute disclaimer prior to contract acceptance. This is one instance where, no matter how firm the disclaimer, the parties will go ahead and do as they please anyway. Make your disclaimer very clear. When the trouble starts, everyone is going to try to point to the broker.

Fraud and the Government Loan

With the tendency of the federal government agencies, especially the FHA and the VA, to be apparently unresponsive and unaware of what is happening in the world, some people have decided that the regulations that govern such loans are like the fifty-five mile speed limit, ineffective, unrealistic, often unenforced, and carrying a little penalty when adjudicated. Let me assure you that although these giants appear to have a hard time getting anything accomplished and appear oblivious to the transgressions that are occurring, they have enlisted, in addition to their own in-house staff of overworked investigators, a cadre of FBI agents and the offices of the U.S. Attorney to assist in their search for and prosecution of those that are defrauding the government.

Some real estate licensees still are trying to have someone obtain an "owner occupant" loan when in fact the prospective borrower never intends to live in the property. Others have determined that a new FHA loan makes the property much more salable and therefore are encouraging sellers to refinance and then sell the property. Yet another group is encouraging people to refinance and immediately sell to a buyer procured prior to the refinance. While these courses of conduct vary in their abuse of the rules and the law, they do not hold a candle to the outright abuses advanced by some people.

The professional broker and agent, while never engaging in such activities, may be caught in the ever-expanding net thrown to capture the true offenders. Care needs to be taken in even the most routine transaction involving government loans to insure that everything is properly completed. When the pressure starts, the buyer and seller know who is responsible, the broker.

The following case in point, while not exactly indicative of the foregoing, exemplifies the ramifications of what appears to be a normal transaction for a hectic agent.

Case in Point

The hurried, experienced agent (ten years plus in the business) answers a call on an advertisement for the sale of a friend's property. A smooth showing results in a contract indicating a new VA loan. The agent takes the buyer to the lender who "does all my business." The loan goes through the normal process and is approved and ready to close. But a delay in funding forces the lender to reverify the employment of the purchaser. The call to the employer results in the reply: "He has never worked for my husband."

The lender contacts the agent who talks with the buyer who assures the agent that all is well; he just does not get along with the spouse of the boss. The agent, believing the buyer he barely knows, suggests to the lender that it is all a mistake. The lender calls the VA who comes to see the agent. Believing that the truth is a good defense and easily noticed by trained investigators, the real estate agent talks to the investigating agents, who include an FBI agent, and explains all he knows.

The result is that the agent is involved in a grand jury investigation which almost leads to his being indicted on several felony counts. The buyer, who never was employed by anyone, had sent the verification to himself. When confronted by the investigators, the buyer replied, "The agent thought up the entire scam."

Fortunately, the investigators also later talked with the friend-employer. The agent, poorer now from attorney's fees but still married, sane and alive pleads guilty to a misdemeanor and bargains for two years probation, not because he is guilty, but because he cannot win. During that time the agent will not be allowed to be involved in any VA loans.

The good news is that the prohibition against being involved in VA loans is reduced to only those transactions involving the agent. Formerly, it had been anyone associated with the agent. How could an office list property in good faith if VA financing was not an alternative for any buyer or seller.

The result was that a very good real estate professional almost lost it all. The lessons: know at least a little about your buyer; maybe make a call to the place of work; realize that through the efforts of a terrible few, government loans are under attack and your reputation, a reputation made one deal at a time over a long period of time, may be the only thing that can save you when the going gets tough. In this case, a good reputation was one of the deciding factors.

Mr. Gary S. Joiner
Mrs. Karen A. Joiner
4750 Table Mesa Drive
Boulder, CO 80303

    Re: 75 McCoy Drive, Windhaven

Dear Mr. and Mrs. Joiner:

    With the market in its current condition and the attractive terms already in place in the loan that you currently have on your property, there is a good possibility that we will receive an offer which requests that you allow the assumption of your existing loan. You indicated in your Listing Agreement that this was an acceptable alternative. Because of the long-term nature of this arrangement, I would like to review the differences between the "Assumption" of the existing debt, the taking of the property "Subject To" the existing debt and a "Novation." Please review it now so that you will be familiar with the differences prior to receiving an offer that poses one of these alternatives. As the law is constantly changing in this area, you may wish to seek legal advice. This is a good topic to discuss with your real estate attorney.

    First, let's review the process of "Assumption." Our attorney has advised us that when someone such as you allow your loan to be assumed, the buyer promises you that he will pay the lender, thereby promising to discharge the loan according to its terms. At this point, the buyer is personally liable to the lender and to you to complete that obligation. You remain liable for the repayment personally. [Should the buyer not perform, you remain liable for the repayment of the obligation.] If the lender commences a foreclosure, it could prove detrimental to your credit. This is a strange area since some lenders do not adversely reflect upon the credit of the original and intermediate borrowers, concentrating instead on the last person in line to formally, properly, assume the loan. Other lenders, however, do look to the original borrower. There seems to be no standard procedure. In the event of a foreclosure sale that is insufficient to fully retire the loan, some states allow the lender to commence a suit against all who are obligated on the note for the deficiency, while other states expressly prohibit such deficiency judgment actions. Colorado allows deficiency judgments and all lenders, with the notable recent addition of FHA, are currently reviewing their loans to determine if such an action is justified.

When you allow your property to be transferred "Subject To" the loan, there is no personal obligation on the part of the buyer to pay the loan. The loan gets paid because the buyer knows that if it does not get paid the lender will probably foreclose and take the property away from the buyer. You remain liable personally for the ultimate repayment, just as indicated in the assumption option, the buyer simply agrees to take title to the property with your existing loan in place.

A "Novation" occurs when the lender releases you from your personal obligation of and liability for the repayment of the loan and substitutes the new buyer. The original loan remains in place, just like the other alternatives. However, the lender, usually after qualifying the buyer, agrees that in the future the lender will look only to the new buyer and not to you for repayment. This may sound like the best solution, but it is not often a reality because the lender wants all the borrowers it can get to remain personally liable for the repayment of your loan. To require a novation will eliminate your liability in much the same manner as if the buyer had obtained a new loan. It will also greatly reduce your ability to sell your home since one of the attractive features of your existing financing is the fact that the loan can be assumed without any qualification or with the limited approval of the lender. The decision is a hard one and only you can make it.

In either event, your loan could go into foreclosure and you would be powerless, as a practical matter, to stop the foreclosure and recover the property from your buyer or from a subsequent purchaser. While you always have the opportunity to pay the lender, the ability to recover the property might involve a lawsuit and all the requisite delays and expenses associated therewith. This is simply a function of today's real estate market and the legal system. There is not an easy answer to this dilemma; although, legal advice may help you understand everything a little better.

If you would like to discuss this matter further with either Jim or me, please feel free to give one of us a call at any time. Financing is one of the more complicated aspects of modern real estate transactions and needs to be given careful consideration. We want to insure that all our clients and customers have an ample opportunity to learn about, understand, and explore all the available options.

Most sincerely,
Denver Canadian Realty, Inc.

Lee D. Weinstein

by: Lee D. Weinstein, Broker

Seller Financing—Creative Financing

This is probably the most dangerous area of the real estate transaction and yet an absolute necessity in many of today's transactions. For a great many sellers and buyers, all the ramifications of a particular seller-financed transaction are simply never explained, let alone understood. Care should be taken to explain the entire transaction, not only orally but also in writing, and to indicate in advance all of the alternatives to and ramifications of the proposed financing. It is imperative to realize that the broker and salesperson are for all practical purposes practicing law in this area and, therefore, will be held to the standard of an attorney. Danger lurks as the documents written or completed by the broker will last longer than the memory of the most conscientious of the agents and parties.

Terms and Conditions

The Checklist may seem endless, but you should recognize that several items are imperative.

1. **Interest.** Double-check the normal ("face") interest rate and default interest rate that will accrue. Are the rates fixed or variable and if variable what index are they tied to?

2. **Late Charges.** Explain the existence, amount of, and effective date for a late charge. Remember, a late charge can only be collected once on each payment, not once for each month the payment remains unpaid.

3. **Dates, Amount, Application.** Cover all the dates and payment application, spelling out the dates on which the payments will become due and the amount of each of the payments; the date and amount of non-periodic payments; the application or allocation between principal and interest—of all payments.

4. **Escrow.** Note the inclusion of an additional amount for an escrow for taxes and insurance. Note also the extent of the services and responsibilities of the escrow agent. Never become, or allow yourself to be coerced into becoming, an escrow agent. There is always a greater fool, a title company, a bank, a neighbor, or someone else for the job. Explain the rate of interest, if any, that will accrue upon the funds in escrow or the allocation of any escrow charges with regard to the escrow account. If no one is designated as being responsible for the monthly fee, we know who will get to pay it: the real estate broker. So share the fun and designate some other deserving party.

5. **Prepayment.** Detail the ability to prepay, the minimum amount of any prepayment and the timing of a prepayment. Some sellers may not be able to accept a prepayment for tax reasons. Unless specified in the note to the contrary, there is no right to prepay.

6. **Assumption.** Specify whether or not the loan is assumable and, if so, under what conditions. Unless specified otherwise, all loans are assumable. The word "assumability" is a misnomer. What one really means is: Does the loan to contain a due-on-sale clause? Confusion here is to be avoided. Any method of qualifying a new borrower that calls for the subjective approval of the seller is to be avoided. Idea: Make the loan due-on-sale until the principal balance is reduced to a certain figure; thereafter, allow a transfer so long as the loan is assumed. Consider the inclusion of a clause providing for the increase in the interest rate upon each transfer.

7. **Common Sense.** Can the seller really do without the money? Ask also, is this a good investment for the seller, especially given the current rates available in certificates of deposit? Although it is not your job to do planning for a seller, a thirty-year fixed rate loan comprising all of the assets of an elderly seller might cause one to pause and encourage the intervention of a trusted accountant, priest, or an attorney.

7. **Foreclosure.** Make clear the effect upon the seller if the buyer stops making the payments. Does the seller understand the foreclosure alternatives, the cost, the time delay, the possible outcome? Many older sellers think that the buyer does not own the house until the debt is paid. They confuse a transaction which transfers title by deed with the seller retaining a security interest in the form of a deed of trust or mortgage with an installment land contract.

8. **Form Selection and Terms.** The best solution I have ever found is to annex the owner carry-back note and deed of trust, or other financing documents, completed in as much detail as possible, as an exhibit to the sales contract. That way there is no confusion about what was actually intended or which forms will be utilized.

Side Agreements

The use of the term alone should start the conscience of most real estate professionals wondering. Why is there an agreement that cannot be a part of the contract? I know of no answer other than that the facts expressed in the side agreement are to be concealed from someone who, had they known all of the facts of the proposed transaction, would have reacted in a fashion different from what was intended—also often referred to as "Criminal Fraud on a Federally Chartered or Insured Lender."

With the exception of such obvious motivations such as keeping a relative or mother-in-law from knowing where you are moving or the purchasing of commercial property as an undisclosed agent, there are very few times when any side agreement is appropriate. This is a good area to avoid. The "If I do not see it, it does not exist" theory, the ostrich theory, offers no safe haven. Once you know of an irregularity, you are under several often-conflicting duties to report to the lender, the government, the seller, the buyer, your board and, always, your broker. Do not be a coconspirator.

Case in Point

The listing agent, who is a friend of the wife of a client-couple involved in a divorce, agrees to list the property for one commission and rebate a portion of the commission to the wife. The other seller, the husband, has no knowledge of this "side agreement." Is that not fraud? Are not both the sellers your clients?

The final straw is the agent's remark when questioned. He said, "I just wanted to help the wife. You know we have been friends for a long time."

Remember that the fiduciary duty is owed by an agent to all the principals?

Offer Proposing Owner Financing

DENVER CANADIAN
REALTY, INC.
420 Ponderosa Drive   Boulder, CO 80303
(303) 494-6661

Mr. Gary S. Joiner
Mrs. Karen A. Joiner
4750 Table Mesa Drive
Boulder, CO 80303

Re: 75 McCoy Drive, Windhaven

Dear Mr. and Mrs. Joiner:

As you know by now, we are happy to have an offer on your home for your consideration. This particular offer, like all others, needs to be carefully reviewed to determine if it suits your needs. It is important that you fully understand the implications of the transaction as it is proposed, so feel free to contact me at any time to further explain the ramifications of the transaction as proposed by the buyer.

Obligation to Present all Offers

Please understand that we are obligated by law to present directly to you for consideration any and all offers that are delivered to us. Although it would be nice to empower us to make the initial determination, that is simply not the law, nor is it the policy of this office. You, and you alone, are the decision maker. No matter how far-fetched or unworkable the offer may at first seem, it is still a written indication that someone wants to find out if there is a possible avenue for the acquisition of your property.

Owner-Carry Financing

Please note that this offer proposes that you will lend the buyer some money as part of the purchase price in the form of a second note and deed of trust. Your position will be junior to that of the existing first mortgage lender, and, therefore, your rights will be subject to that senior lender's rights. A failure to make the payments on the senior mortgage may make it difficult for you to reclaim the property fast enough to realize on your security.

As I am sure you can understand, we are professionals in obtaining buyers but do not have the expertise to determine their current financial qualifications. Nor can we determine whether or not they will meet their obligations now or in the future, should you decide to extend financing. We simply cannot be responsible for the creditworthiness or the present or future performance of the buyer. I am amazed at the complex nature of the credit reporting system; and, although we encourage you to obtain a financial statement and credit report, we must direct you to other professionals to interpret these documents. I have found that the use of your local banker or a trip to the credit bureau with the buyer will provide you with some insight into the qualifications of the buyer and what additional documents might be necessary to help determine the creditworthy nature of the buyer.

Note that the proposed instruments to evidence the debt and secure its repayment have been annexed to and included in the contract, should you decide to accept the buyer's offer and provide the requested financing. This is the time to review and understand these documents. I would be willing to explain them in general to you and also encourage you, if you so desire, to seek the advice of a real estate lawyer to assist you with the final decision. If you would like me to go along, I would be happy to help explain the transaction.

General Assignment of Tasks

Should you decide to accept this offer, there are a number of items that we will require of everyone in order to accomplish the objective of a timely closing. Some we accept responsibility for, some are the buyer's obligation, and the remaining tasks are your responsibility. To assist everyone in determining who has the responsibility for each item, I have enclosed a list showing the tasks, the party that needs to complete each item, and the completion date for each item. Please consult the list and advise us if you need additional help with any of your responsibilities. Although we cannot guarantee the performance of the other parties, we will endeavor to assist them in every reasonable way possible to get their tasks completed in a timely fashion.

No home is ever sold until it closes. We realize that you are going to make some tentative commitments based on the contract as accepted, so we want to remind you that there are a lot of circumstances that must occur before the closing transpires. Be careful not to overcommit your resources until we actually close.

We are on the way to closing and I want to thank you for always having your home in such nice condition. I know the neat clean appearance took some extra time and effort, but I am sure it was a factor in attracting this buyer.

Most sincerely,
Denver Canadian Realty, Inc.

Lee D. Weinstein

by: Lee D. Weinstein, Broker

DENVER CANADIAN
REALTY, INC.
420 Ponderosa Drive   Boulder, CO 80303
(303) 494-6661

Mr. Gary S. Joiner
Mrs. Karen A. Joiner
4750 Table Mesa Drive
Boulder, CO 80303

    Re: 75 McCoy Drive, Windhaven

Dear Mr. and Mrs. Joiner:

As you know by now, we are happy to have an offer on your home for your consideration. This particular offer, like all others, needs to be carefully reviewed to determine if it will suit your needs. Even though not exactly what you had requested, it deserves careful consideration. In a market such as this one, no reasonable offer needs to be dismissed. It is important that you fully understand the implications of the transaction as it is proposed. Feel free, therefore, to call on me at any time to explain the ramifications of the proposal.

Please note that this offer proposes that your existing loan with Wells Fargo Credit Corporation be assumed by the buyer. Assumption is a promise by the buyer to pay your note and mortgage with Wells Fargo, according to its terms. Two items need your review:

First, the note and mortgage require that the buyer apply through the Wells Fargo Credit Corporation for, and be approved for, the assumption of the loan and the transfer of the property as proposed in the contract. This procedure keeps the lender from exercising its right to call the loan all due and payable in full, or due-on-sale. Do not place too great a significance upon the lender's approval of the buyer for the assumption. Although we will request a novation, that is, the release of your personal obligation to repay the note, it is not currently a condition of the contract. Pressing too hard for one could undermine the transaction as proposed and is rarely given by this lender.

Second, as this is an assumption, unless the lender agrees to the contrary, both you and the buyer will be jointly and severally liable for the repayment of the loan. In the event the buyer or his successor in interest does not make the payments, the lender has the option to seek payment in full from you. We do not know the effect that this might have on your credit. You will probably not be able to obtain a voluntary reconveyance of the property from the purchaser or his successor in interest.

Transfer Without Prior Lender Approval

You and the buyer have agreed, in spite of our advice to the contrary, that neither of you will seek the approval of the holder of the loan, Wells Fargo Credit Corporation. That is, of course, your decision. Please understand that neither this office nor anyone associated with it, including but not limited to James C. Smittkamp and me, can be responsible or liable for any action taken by Wells Fargo or anyone else, or for any other ramifications of this transaction that may arise as a result of your following this course of action. These ramifications could include a foreclosure action and/or your being named in a lawsuit upon the note. You are advised to seek the advice of an attorney before embarking on such a course of action.

FHA Release of Liability

Since this is an FHA loan, there is an option granted by some lenders holding FHA insured loans to remove you from liability and substitute the new buyer. We will again try to determine if this lender will allow such a substitution. You remember that our initial investigation at the time of the listing was inconclusive on this point because the lender indicated that they could not commit until the loan was actually in the assumption department. Do not get your hopes up. Most often there is no option for the substitution of the new buyer to replace you.

All-Inclusive (Wrap Around) Financing

One possible option that you may or may not remember that I indicated to you when we listed your home is that you accept an all-inclusive obligation. Simply put, this would mean that the buyer would execute a note, secured by a deed of trust for the entire amount of your existing loan. The buyer would pay you on a monthly basis and you would in turn remit the same amount to the underlying, existing lender. This would reserve for you the option to foreclose upon your All-Inclusive Deed of Trust and obtain the return to you of the property without disturbing the underlying loan by allowing an assumption. If this is interesting to you, we can explore it in more detail. It is an effective tool when the underlying financing does not have a due-on-sale clause, as is the case with some FHA loans and generally true under the existing VA loan conditions.

[In some states, the objective indicated is accomplished with an All-Inclusive Deed of Trust, in others an All-Inclusive Mortgage, and finally in some states through an Installment Land Contract or Contract for Deed, which differs only in the fact that the title does not transfer until the contract has been fully completed, usually paid in full. Nevertheless, the theory is the same, the seller remains in control of the existing or underlying financing until some condition is met.]

VA-Substitution of Eligibility

Even though this is a VA loan and the buyer is a veteran, the release of your personal obligation to pay and the substitution of the buyer requires that the buyer also have a VA entitlement and that he qualify for the loan, similar in most respects to a new loan application. The attractive aspect of your loan is that it can be assumed without the need to qualify and without the need to pay the extra expenses associated with obtaining new financing, such as discount points and loan origination fees.

Unfortunately the prospective buyer is not a veteran, and, therefore, this option is not available. Even if it were, one of the attractive features is the existing loan assumption that we have discussed earlier. Such a substitution is similar to a new loan and, therefore, would require the normal processing time and qualification procedure.

As we discussed, you may want to make the contract conditional upon your being released of liability on the first loan. If you want to make such a release a condition of the contract, it needs to be inserted into the contract before you sign and accept the offer.

Effect of a Counterproposal

This offer is capable of acceptance in its present condition. Any changes that are made, either by crossing out a term and initialing it or by executing a counter proposal, give the other party the opportunity to walk away from the transaction with impunity. Such a counterproposal is a rejection of the original offer and a proposal of a different offer back to the buyer. There is nothing that compels the buyer to consider or accept the counterproposal. Once a counterproposal has been, the original offer is no longer capable of acceptance in its original form. With that in mind, let me encourage you to review each proposed change to determine if it is critical to the transaction before making the change to the offer.

As always, the advice of an attorney is recommended. If I can be of assistance in explaining the alternatives to you and/or your attorney, accountant, priest or other advisor, please do not hesitate to call. If you do not have an advisor, just do what I tell you. I have always wanted to be sued, hire lawyers, and go to court, just like on television. This is an important point in the sale and you need to feel comfortable in your understanding of the alternatives and in your ultimate decision.

It is a pleasure to be your listing agent for the sale of your property. If there is anything that I can do to assist you please do not hesitate to let me know.

Most sincerely,
Denver Canadian Realty, Inc.

Lee D. Weinstein

by: Lee D. Weinstein, Broker

DENVER CANADIAN
REALTY, INC.
420 Ponderosa Drive   Boulder, CO 80303
(303) 494-6661

Mr. Albert A. Desperate
Mrs. Martha B. Desperate
6990 Hopeless Avenue
Madison, MN 90303

Mr. Wilber C. Hungry
Mrs. Freda D. Hungry
Apartment 210 A
West End Apartments
999 Last Avenue
Madison, MN 80303

     Re: 6990 Hopeless Avenue
        Desperation City

Dear Mr. and Mrs. Desperate and Mr. and Mrs. Hungry:

I know that both of you are anticipating this letter and I am sorry that I have to write it. I simply have no other option than to formally clarify my position and that of this office with regard to the transaction that you are proposing. Please understand our position and review this letter carefully.

As I indicated to you both over the phone today and in person over the last two days, your joint decision to allow the sellers to apply for and utilize their credit to obtain a new FHA loan as owner occupants, with the intention that, as soon as the loan is obtained and closed they will transfer the property to the purchasers and allow an assumption of that new FHA loan, is a violation of the rules and regulations promulgated by the Department of Housing and Urban Development. Neither I nor this office can be a party to such a transaction.

We understand your respective desperate needs to sell and buy the home in question and we are not passing on the validity of the transaction, only that it violates the regulations as we understand them. You are, of course, free to take whatever action you desire. We would advise you to seek the closing services of a title company or other suitable closing agent to insure that the transaction's financial calculations are properly accounted for. In addition, we would advise you again to seek the services of a real estate attorney or to contact the FHA directly to fully understand the ramifications of the transaction you propose.

There is no doubt that the purchaser was procured by the efforts of this office and, should the transaction close, we will be entitled to receive our commission, indicated in the listing agreement. There is no requirement that we draft the contract or conduct the closing, only that we provide you with a purchaser acceptable to you or that you transfer the property to a purchaser that was procured by us.

I know that you understand our position and we appreciate your respecting the fact that we cannot be a part of the transaction as you propose it. Nevertheless, congratulations on the pending purchase and sale of this property.

As with any assumption, there is a potential for damage to be inflicted to the credit of both parties in the event that the loan payments are not timely made. Reference should be made to the pamphlet we have given you both, "Assumption, Subject To and Novation, Your Liabilities and Rights".

Most sincerely,
Denver Canadian Realty, Inc.

James C. Smittkamp

by: James C. Smittkamp, Salesperson

cc: Lee D. Weinstein, Broker
    Oliver E. Frascona, Esq.

DENVER CANADIAN
REALTY, INC.
420 Ponderosa Drive   Boulder, CO 80303
(303) 494-6661

Mr. Gary S. Joiner
Mrs. Karen A. Joiner
4750 Table Mesa Drive
Boulder, CO 80303

    Re: 75 McCoy Drive, Windhaven

Dear Gary and Karen:

    With this letter, we are happy to include an offer that exactly meets the terms and conditions you requested in your Listing Agreement. This kind of offer is always nice to present. It is important that you fully understand the implications of the transaction as proposed by the offer so feel free to contact me immediately to explain the ramifications of the proposed transaction. As always, should you feel you need it, the advice of an attorney is recommended.

    Few people are capable of paying all cash, so I have insisted that the earnest money be equal to five percent of the total sales price. It is rare to obtain such a substantial amount of earnest money. Although all indications are that it will be a quick closing within the next few weeks, I never consider a property sold until the actual closing, with the funds having been paid and having cleared the bank. [Contrary to popular opinion, even certified funds must clear and are subject to stop payment orders.] I would advise you not to irrevocably obligate yourselves based upon this contract until it actually closes.

               Most sincerely,
               Denver Canadian Realty, Inc.

               James C. Smittkamp

               by: James C. Smittkamp, Salesperson

cc: Lee D. Weinstein, Broker

Offer Proposing New Financing

DENVER CANADIAN
REALTY, INC.
420 Ponderosa Drive   Boulder, CO 80303
(303) 494-6661

Mr. Gary S. Joiner
Mrs. Karen A. Joiner
4750 Table Mesa Drive
Boulder, CO 80303

Re: 75 McCoy Drive, Windhaven

Dear Gary and Karen:

The news we have all been waiting for has arrived. This letter contains an offer from Jon and Mimi Goodman. The terms are not exactly what you wanted but they are very close. Review the offer as quickly as possible because it expires tomorrow at midnight. While it is always possible for a buyer to withdraw an offer before it is accepted, I think the Goodmans want you to consider their offer very seriously. They spent a good deal of time working on their financing so that they felt they could afford to present the offer.

This offer indicates that the buyers' obligations are conditional upon their being able to obtain a new first loan in the amount of $256,000.00, a 77% loan-to-value ratio, using their proposed contract price. While there is a risk that they cannot qualify for the financing, there are very few buyers who can either pay cash or enter into a contract without such a loan condition. You will note that the application must be made by Tuesday of next week and the loan approved on or before July 25, 1987. Thereafter, the earnest money could be in jeopardy. It is impossible for us to determine if any buyer will qualify for the proposed loan. In this instance, I have asked that the buyer present a financial statement and work history with the offer so that you can try to determine if they are a good risk.

Your home will be effectively off the market while the loan application is in process. Although we can continue to solicit backup offers, the news that a house is under contract discourages others from trying to purchase it.

Payoff Penalty

A new loan will cause your old loan to be paid off in full which may trigger the payoff penalty that we discussed earlier. One good aspect of such a payoff is the termination of your personal liability for the repayment of that loan. If you wish to require that the buyer try first to get a loan from Friendly Federal Savings and Loan Association in order to possibly avoid that penalty, that provision will need to be inserted in a counterproposal before the contract can become a firm and final deal. The buyer then has the following options: accepting the counterproposal, rejecting the entire transaction, or making another offer.

Once you have made the counterproposal, the buyers can accept it with their signature. I told the Goodmans of your desire that they try to obtain their new loan through Friendly Federal before they wrote their offer. They seemed to feel that the interest rates and terms at Empire Savings and Loan were more to their liking. Thought needs to be given to making any counter-proposal because it gives the buyers time to reconsider and maybe change their mind.

Jim will explain the offer in detail and both of us are always available for discussion should you wish to review the offer at any time in more detail. It is great to have this opportunity to serve you. The final decision is yours.

Most sincerely,
Denver Canadian Realty, Inc.

Lee D. Weinstein

by: Lee D. Weinstein, Broker

Mr. Gary S. Joiner
Mrs. Karen A. Joiner
4750 Table Mesa Drive
Boulder, CO 80303

    Re: 75 McCoy Drive, Windhaven

Dear Mr. and Mrs. Joiner:

    As you know by now, we are happy to have an offer on your home for your consideration. It has been a difficult job to market your home because of the glut of other homes in your price range on the market. There are just too many to choose from. We really appreciate your efforts to always have the home ready to show even on a few moments' notice. I really believe the purchasers selected this home because of the superb condition of the property, and you deserve the credit for your efforts.

    This offer indicates that the buyer will have to sell and close upon his present home in Vail before he will be obligated to purchase your home. This imposes some degree of risk because the contract for the sale of the buyer's current home has its own potential problems. I have insisted that a copy of that contract be attached to the offer so that you can review it in detail. In addition, I have contacted the agent who is assisting the buyer in the purchase of the Vail house and indicated that you and I will probably be calling to discuss the status of that transaction. The buyers, Dave and Joan Farus, have indicated that you are more than welcome to speak with their agent as well as with their subagent, if it will help you decide to accept their offer. Their office and home telephones follow:

    Subagent assisting the buyers of the Farus home:
Jim Rodenbeek, The Rodenbeek Agency
Scott City, Kansas (316) 872-5134

Mr. and Mrs. Farus' agent:
Bill Henderson, The Cibolo Creek Company
499-8724

Most people who will be able to afford your home are the owners of an existing house. The sale of their current residence, although sometimes not indicated in the contract, is going to be the deciding factor in the approval process of the new lender. The lender also then will probably make the closing of the current home a condition of loan approval.

As with any offer, even ones that have no indicated conditions, there is a degree of uncertainty until the deal actually closes. It is with this in mind that we caution you not to rely too heavily on this particular sale until it is final. We cannot be responsible for actions or inactions that are not within our control, and the abilities and intentions of a buyer are definitely outside of our control. Although we will try hard to keep ourselves abreast of the events as they unfold, we cannot make the decisions for any of the parties.

This particular offer, like any other legally binding contract, needs to be carefully reviewed to determine if it suits your needs. It is important that you fully understand the implications of the transaction as it is proposed, so please feel free to ask me at any time to further explain the ramifications of the proposed transaction. We cannot give legal advice, and, therefore, you may wish to use an attorney for that purpose. We can, however, explain the contract in detail so that you can make an informed decision.

We would be happy to accompany you to the attorney's office to help review the contract if you wish. If you decide not to select an attorney, we will just do his job without compensation; and, in the event we do not meet your expectations, you can feel free to sue us. Our contracts are so poorly drafted that we are nervous about having you take them to an attorney. In addition, since you never really agreed to anything in the contract and are so unsure of the transaction, not really needing a place to live anyway, we are very suspect of you taking the contract to anyone to review it. If you are such a simple-minded fool to let some lawyer talk you out of the deal, there is really no need to go see one. I can just take care of the details he would normally attend to, such as reviewing the title commitment, only to find that the seller does not really own the property, and only finding that out now because I was too lazy to order a commitment before I sold you the property. Plus, I can also give you erroneous financial and tax advice.

I know I speak for the entire staff when I say that we have enjoyed having your home in our inventory. I think the Faruses are excited to be buying your house and that good feeling is certainly a nice help in keeping them interested through the rigorous loan application, qualification, and closing processes.

Most sincerely,
Denver Canadian Realty, Inc.

Lee D. Weinstein

by: Lee D. Weinstein, Broker

cc: Bar Association
Unauthorized Practice Section
Real Estate Commission

Chapter Five

After the Contract is Signed

Contract Progress

Contract is Signed

At some point, whether after the initial offer, or after one or more counteroffers, the final document is signed and the real estate professional feels that there is a contract. Communicating this fact, that the final document has been signed, rather than that there is a contract, is necessary to the transaction. Presenting the facts and allowing the parties to draw their own conclusions is the best way to be professional.

Removal of Conditions Precedent

As each of the conditions listed in the contract is satisfied, it is important to notify the parties of this progress. Again, notification of the fact that an item has been removed or satisfied is better than drawing a conclusion as to the effect of the removal. This is a good stage to send copies of a letter addressed to one party to the other parties. Careful structure here can be an adroit way to accomplish your objectives.

Title Insurance Commitment Arrival

In most contracts, it is important to insure that the buyer receives and receipts for the title insurance commitment prior to the date specified in the contract. Once this has occurred, everyone needs to be notified. There have been attempts by the courts to make the selling agent an agent of the buyer in order to correct a default when the title insurance makes it to the selling agent but not to the buyer within the alloted time.

Notification serves two purposes: First, it confirms that the commitment was actually delivered; and second, it puts the recipient on notice that, in the event the notification is defective, he had better speak up or there will arise a presumption that the notification was correct. Secure this by using the silent response technique in your letter as outlined in the early part of this book.

Loan Application and Commitment

In each case, when the buyer has commenced an application or when she has been approved for the loan, communicate the information firmly to the other party. Often this is first done by telephone; however, a follow up letter will avoid a lot of problems with the timing and content of the telephone conversation.

Cover letters to lenders are becoming a necessity. The market changes quickly. Pressure on the loan officers to make deals and attract business are extreme, as are the pressures to make that business profitable. The memories of all players are taxed to the maximum. A simple cover letter with the appropriate copies can help to redefine the deal, keep good business friends happy, and protect yourself, as well as informing the other parties of the exact contents of the quote or commitment. Think for a minute: Who can lock in the rate? The buyer, the seller, someone's agent?

DENVER CANADIAN
REALTY, INC.
420 Ponderosa Drive   Boulder, CO 80303
(303) 494-6661

Mr. and Mrs. Jonathan A. Goodman
Apartment 610 A
12th and Main Street
Denver, CO 80303

    Re: 909 East First Street
        Pagosa Springs, CO

Dear Mr. and Mrs. Goodman:

As you have probably heard, your offer on 909 East First Street was signed [accepted] by the seller this Tuesday at 10:00 P.M. Congratulations on the purchase of your new home. There are many things that need to be done to get ready for the closing and possession of the home. In order to let everyone know who has what responsibility, let me outline the various assignments for all concerned.

First, you will need to apply within the next five days for a loan fitting the minimum parameters of the contract, i.e., a loan amount of $45,000.00, an interest rate of 10% per annum amortized over thirty years. Frank has provided you with a partial list of lenders who have elected to have their rates and other information included in the list and who are currently doing business in this area. Although not exhaustive, it should give you a good place to start. As always, the ultimate selection of a lender is your decision. We recommend that you call a few lenders for rate quotes and then select one or two for your initial application. Each has its own programs and alternatives in addition to the standard government (VA and FHA) loans.

We have learned that purchasers like to discuss their finances with a loan officer of their choice and let that lender assist them in making the personal determination of the exact type, terms, and amount of loan that will suit their needs. For this reason, we do not attempt to counsel anyone concerning the right loan for their needs. When you have selected a lender and made a loan appointment, please let us know so that we can assist you and that lender in gathering the information and documentation that the lender requires. To assist you in preparing for the initial interview, I have enclosed a partial list of information often requested so that you can gather as much of it as possible in advance and expedite the application process.

Second, you will need to select a home inspection service and termite inspection service, as well as a moving company. While many home inspection services are available, we have included a list of services used by previous customers for your review. We have found that a good mover is Happy Land Lines and recommend them highly. [Used when part of a referral service.]

Third, you will need to decide on the educational alternatives available. A list of the public and private schools within a reasonable distance from your new home is included. It has been so long since any of us attended school that an opinion on the quality or availability of various educational services would not be reliable. Each person evaluates the needs of their children and the various offerings of each school system differently. It is a personal choice. Please note the phone number of the school board. They are available to assist you and can provide answers to your questions in the future.

You will need to complete the first item by Monday, the 20th, and the others within the next two weeks. Remember, the closing date is set for Friday, the 15th of March, and you will need to have your funds available. To speed the obtaining of the balance of the down payment, I would suggest opening a local bank account at your earliest convenience. We do our business directly with the Federal Reserve Bank and would be glad to introduce you to Mr. Paul Volker, the president, if you desire. There are other banks and savings and loan associations in the area, and I am sure that whoever you initially select will be able to get you started with an account and provide you with certified funds for closing.

Thank you for letting us serve [help] you in viewing and selecting the home of your choice. It is nice to have you as customers. Your daughter will love the pink room with the teddy bear wallpaper.

Most sincerely,
Denver Canadian Realty, Inc.

Lee D. Weinstein

by: Lee D. Weinstein, Broker

Mr. and Mrs. Jonathan A. Goodman
Apartment 610 A
12th and Main Street
Denver, CO 80303

    Re: 909 East First Street

Dear Mr. and Mrs. Goodman:

Title Commitment

There continue to be fewer tasks that need to be accomplished as the closing day approaches. I am happy to enclose a copy of the Title Insurance Commitment obtained from Trautwein Title and Abstract Company. It looks like we obtained and delivered it to you just prior to the target date in the contract. Review it carefully and talk with the title officer indicated or with Cindy Trautwein, the manager, if you have any questions. The lender will also probably review it for their own purposes to assure that they are happy. You should not allow the lender's acceptance of the commitment to influence your determination of its sufficiency since the lender has no obligation to you with regard to their determination of the adequacy of the commitment.

Form 130

As I indicated to you early on, and as indicated in the contract, I ordered and have obtained a Form 130 Endorsement for you which will offer some protection against mechanics' liens, unrecorded documents and other items indicated in the standard commitment. Be sure to address that endorsement when you talk to the title officer. Her number is 449-7500. Review the extent of the Form 130 coverage with the title company to your satisfaction. Although Trautwein Title and Abstract Company seems to enjoy a good reputation, we cannot be responsible for their title insurance, commitments, policies, actions or inactions, nor for the condition of the title because we simply are not licensed title examiners.

The lender has ordered and completed the appraisal that the lender requires to determine whether they will make the loan you have requested. Although you pay for the appraisal, it is the property of the lender, and they will generally neither divulge the amount that was indicated nor give it to you because they have indicated previously that they feel that it is for their information only. The good news is that it is sufficient to allow the loan to proceed forward to loan committee.

VA Loan Appraisal

Since the loan you are obtaining is a VA loan, the lender must give you a copy of the appraisal performed by the appraiser, who is endorsed by the Veterans Administration. It indicates that the value which that appraiser has placed on the property is for loan purposes only and is at least as high as was provided in the contract.

FHA Appraisal is Low

The FHA appraisal has come back a few thousand dollars lower than anticipated. Therefore, you are in a position to either proceed with the purchase as proposed, making up the loan proceeds shortage with additional down payment, or consider the contract as void and let someone else purchase the home. Please let me know of your decision so that I can advise the seller immediately and prepare the necessary addendum or release form.

Survey

The survey required by the lender is not a pin survey but a more cursory survey, by which the surveyor simply determines that in fact the house is on the lot and roughly in the proper position. It is not intended to be relied upon for any other uses, such as the exact location of any of the improvements or easements or the like in reference to other items. There is no substitute for a boundary survey if you are going to build additions or want an accurate determination of the physical condition of the property. As we discussed, that is not a requirement for the loan and is not included in the expenses of the seller as outlined in the contract.

This would be a good time to verify that your mover has the correct date and time of your anticipated move and that your bank has the balance of the amount of your funds needed to complete the transaction on deposit ready and available for closing. The title company will require that the funds be in certified form. I have requested that the title insurance company provide us with the exact amount as soon as possible to facilitate this process.

I'm sure you are happy and excited to be getting close to moving day. It is a real project but when it's over you will be settled in your nice new home. We are glad you selected us to assist you. Please let me know if there is anything I can to do help with the move or in further preparing for the closing.

Most sincerely,
Denver Canadian Realty, Inc.

Lee D. Weinstein

by: Lee D. Weinstein, Broker

Removal of Conditions

DENVER CANADIAN
REALTY, INC.
420 Ponderosa Drive   Boulder, CO 80303
(303) 494-6661

Mrs. and Mr. Gary S. Joiner
4750 Table Mesa Drive
Boulder, CO 80303

Re: 75 McCoy Drive, Windhaven

Dear Gary and Karen:

I am happy to be able to tell you that the purchaser and his engineer went through the property yesterday for their second inspection. As of this date, I have not heard any complaints. The contract provided the following:

"Purchaser, accompanied by such professionals as he alone shall select, shall have the right to inspect the property at the purchaser's expense to determine if the property, in the opinion of the purchaser, is structurally sound. In the event that the purchaser does not indicate to the contrary, the property shall be deemed to be of sound character acceptable to the purchaser. Notice to the contrary must be written, specify the exact details of the deficiency and be delivered to the seller's agent, Denver Canadian Realty, Inc., prior to the 28th of June, 1997."

At this time I am assuming that this condition is no longer a factor. It looks like we are one step closer to the closing. The property shows so nicely, and I know it is a result of your efforts. I appreciate having you for clients.

Sincerely,
Denver Canadian Realty, Inc.

Lee D. Weinstein

by: Lee D. Weinstein, Broker

cc: Mr. Daniel T. Mertz, Subagent
Mr. and Mrs. Jon Goodman, Purchaser
Ms. Trautwein, Trautwein Title and Abstract
Mr. Thomas Richmond, Richmond Mortgage

The Deal Changes

Consideration, The Key

Somewhere along the line, the deal as proposed by the buyer and accepted by the seller may change. Consideration is the key to unlocking this puzzle. Always look to see that each side has altered its obligation in some manner.

Case in Point

The classic case is the one where the builder and owner sign a contract for the construction of a building. Halfway through the construction, the builder announces that there is not enough money to finish the project and that he will quit if the contract cannot be renegotiated. The parties then agree to a new contract for more money. The builder goes back to work and completes the building. When asked to pay the additional amount, the owner refuses and the case goes to court.

The decision: There was no consideration for the revision. The owner was entitled to exactly what he received as outlined in the first contract, and, therefore, the builder provided nothing new in return for the increased price. Lacking additional consideration, the new contract was not enforceable.

Extension and Modification Agreements

Great care should be exercised to recite the additional consideration, if it exists, for the modification or extension of the contract. Generally, if the obligations of both sides are altered, that is enough. The use of the words "this contract supercedes and replaces all previous contracts between the parties for this property" should be used only when that is the intent of the parties. Be careful that all the desired clauses from the first contract make it into the subsequent modified contract. Often it is better to draft a modification agreement, keeping all unchanged parts of the contract intact and only changing some of the terms.

Use of a Contract Modification and Mutual Release Agreement

When the modifications are negotiated in return for some performance or when the parties have made concessions, whether through threat of nonperformance or to settle claims, it is very nice to obtain a final settlement agreement. This is a good place to try to limit the recourse against the broker.

Release Agreements - General Comments and Format

The following is a formal agreement structure. It will look very much like an agreement drafted by a lawyer. To make it more low-key but still effective, leave out the lawyer words, Witnesseth, Whereas, Now Therefore, etc. A title is always a helpful hint for the person who expects a certain document, although it has no real meaning; the content controls.

These agreements contain many provisions that are not needed in the average simple agreement. In addition, there are some nice little clauses for general contract preparation that could be taken from this agreement.

DENVER CANADIAN REALTY, INC.

SAMPLE RELEASE AGREEMENT

THIS AGREEMENT, made and entered into this ____ day of _____, by and between _____ [Here you indicate the effective date, and the names of the parties.] _____;

WITNESSETH:

This, like the WHEREAS that follows, is optional. To include the formal words or not does not effect the document, but it can give one side or the other a certain feeling that you wish to convey as to the formality, finality, and serious nature of the release.

WHEREAS, these are descriptive paragraphs to orient the reader with regard to which transaction is the subject of the release, the things that led up to the settlement, and a little about the dispute. Be concise.

NOW, THEREFORE, each of the parties hereby agrees as follows with the understanding that the other parties are relying upon the representations herein contained, or, for and in consideration of the following promises and conditions, the parties hereby agree as follows: [Now simply insert your recitation that the deal is OK for everyone, that consideration is not a problem, and that the deal follows.]

1. Number each item. Be very specific about what is resolved.

2. Look to the samples below for the needed paragraphs.

IN WITNESS WHEREOF, the signature block needs to contain the same names as the initial heading. Everyone should sign, preferably in your presence.

Party One: Party Two:

_____   _____

DENVER CANADIAN REALTY, INC.

CONTRACT MODIFICATION AND MUTUAL RELEASE AGREEMENT

THIS AGREEMENT, entered into this ＿＿ day of August, 1988, by and between Gary S. Joiner and Karen A. Joiner, ("Seller"); and Jon Goodman and Mimi Goodman ("Buyer"); Denver Canadian Realty, Inc., ("Seller's Broker"), and ＿＿＿＿＿＿＿ ("Other Agent"), all of whom shall constitute the parties ("Parties");

WITNESSETH:

WHEREAS, Seller and Buyer on July 4, 1988, entered into a certain Contract for the Purchase and Sale of Real Estate ("Contract") for the purchase and sale of the property located at 75 McCoy Drive, Windhaven ("Property"); and,

WHEREAS, there is a dispute between the parties with regard to the total square footage of the Property, its value, the items that are to be transferred with the Property, the possession date and the liability for the condition of the Property on and after this date; and,

WHEREAS, a new loan has been obtained by the Buyer, the Property has been inspected by the Buyer and/or the Buyer's authorized agent; and,

WHEREAS, the Parties wish to resolve their disputes as they relate to this contract, specifically but not by way of limitation as they relate to the aforementioned items, and to forever fully release and discharge each other from any and all liability of any nature which may have arisen as a result of the indicated Contract, and the events that followed and provide for the closing and transfer of deed contemplated in the Contract;

NOW, THEREFORE, each of the parties hereby irrevocably covenants, promises and agrees as follows, with the knowledge and intent that the other parties rely on these promises, covenants, agreements and representations:

1. That the Gross Sales Price indicated in the Contract is hereby reduced by the amount of $2,500.00 from $125,500.00 to $123,000.00.

2. That the actual square footage is unknown and not a material part of the transaction.

3. That the date for possession is August 30th, 1988.

4. The items contained in the Bill of Sale are the only items that are being transferred as a part of the Contract, that they have a relative value of $1850.00 and are hereby receipted for by the Buyer in their present condition.

5. That the Buyer has had ample time and opportunity to inspect the Property, and hereby accepts the Property in its present condition, AS IS, WITHOUT ANY WARRANTY, EXPRESS OR IMPLIED, INCLUDING ANY WARRANTY OF FITNESS FOR A PARTICULAR PURPOSE.

6. Except with respect to the enforcement of this Mutual Release, the Parties, for themselves, their heirs, successors and assigns, do hereby remise, release and forever discharge each other, their representatives and agents, servants, officers, directors, heirs, successors, and assigns, of and from any and all claims, actions, causes of action, demands, agreements, damages, costs, promises, expenses and compensation, in law or in equity, known or unknown, which the undersigned Parties, their respective, heirs, successors or assigns, or any of them, may have against one another or which may hereafter accrue or occur, in connection with, on account of, or in any way stemming from any transaction, matter, thing or occurrence the source of which is the Contract, including but not limited to, any and all claims of breach of any contract or agreement whether written or oral, any claims for money had and received, fraud, misrepresentation, negligence, breach of a fiduciary duty, specific performance, and any other claims based on any and all legal or equitable theories upon which a claim for relief or recovery can or could be based.

7. That the parties have each had an opportunity to seek legal counsel and have done so or elected not to do so as their sole and independent act and have not relied in any fashion on any representation made by any party or any agent or employee of any party, for any advice or direction as to the advisability of entering into this Mutual Release.

8. That all parties understand that after this release is executed there will be no opportunity to reevaluate or reopen the matters herein indicated. It being the express purpose of this Mutual Release for everyone to forever completely release the other from any and all claims arising out of the Contract.

9. That in the event any party commences any legal action as a result of this release, whether to enforce it, defend an action based on it or otherwise, the nondefaulting party shall be entitled to a judgment in addition to all

other sums, equal to the nondefaulting party's actual reasonable attorney's fees.

10. This agreement contains the full and complete agreements of the Parties. There are no promises, agreements or representations between any of the Parties except as set forth in this Agreement.

11. This agreement shall be construed under the laws of the State of Colorado, and the Parties agree the venue shall be proper in the District Court located in Boulder County.

12. The singular shall include the plural and the plural the singular. Any references in this Agreement to gender shall include all genders.

13. This Agreement may be executed in counterparts and, in that event, the counterparts, taken together, shall constitute a single instrument.

IN WITNESS WHEREOF, we the undersigned, after having fully read this agreement, hereby execute the same and receipt for a duplicate original of the same on the day and date first above indicated.

Seller: Buyer:

_____   _____
Gary S. Joiner   Jon Goodman

_____   _____
Karen A. Joiner   Mimi Goodman

Seller's Broker: Other Broker:
Denver Canadian Realty, Inc.

By: _____   By: _____
    James C. Smittkamp, Agent   David A. Farus, Broker

Release of Earnest Money

When earnest money has been deposited with the broker and a dispute arises as to the application of the funds, the only way to insure that the broker will be able to distribute the money without the possibility of a future suit is to call for the mutual release by all parties and specify the directions to be followed for the distribution of the funds.

There is no doubt that the pressure will be on from either or both parties, as well as from a buyer's broker or subagent, to have the broker make a determination regarding who is entitled to the money based on a subjective look at the actions or inactions of either or both parties. To let yourself get caught here, no matter what you believe is correct, is an error in judgment and a good time to fall back on "company policy," that is, a mutual release.

Do not let the threat of litigation or the assurance that "everything will be all right" or the promise, no matter how tempting, that one party, usually the seller, will "indemnify you against loss" lull you into a false sense of security. Sure, everybody is going to sue you because you have the money. Get it settled now while you have it. When you have had enough, you can ask the court to take the money and decide who gets how much of it. In addition, you may still reserve your claim to a portion of the money. This is addressed in many of the standard forms. To be effective, the form should indicate that the court "shall," not "may," award attorney's fees to the prevailing party. Courts are wary of having to determine attorney's fees and avoid the imposition of an award for fees unless the contract is specific.

The Mutual Release I have included goes a little far in the release language, but you should be able to pare your own form down a bit. To look legal, it is good to give it a format similar to the one presented; however, a letter format is just as binding. The "Whereas" clauses simply state facts already agreed to and lay the foundation for the solution. You can do this in a letter in any fashion you wish. The "Now, Therefore" clause sets forth the action agreed to and to be taken. Note some of the boiler plate language about reliance. This is nice to have in a release letter.

A form like this can be set up for any mix of parties and agents and is best in a printed and standard-appearing format. Even if it is a special form, title it with a standard label, type it right margin justified, and then copy it so that it does not appear to be special. People sign "standard" forms much more easily than ragged-right, double-spaced letters because there is a sense of correctness about a "standard" form. Use this to your advantage.

DENVER CANADIAN REALTY, INC.

MUTUAL RELEASE AND DISTRIBUTION AGREEMENT

THIS AGREEMENT, entered into this 28th day of June, 1986, by and between Gary S. Joiner and Karen A. Joiner, ("Seller"), and Jon Goodman and Mimi Goodman ("Buyer"), Denver Canadian Realty, Inc., ("Seller's Broker"), and _____ ("Other Agent"), all of whom shall constitute the parties ("Parties");

WITNESSETH:

WHEREAS, Seller and Buyer on _____, 1986 entered into a certain Contract for the Purchase and Sale of Real Estate ("Contract") for the purchase and sale of the property located at 75 McCoy Drive, Windhaven ("Property"); and,

WHEREAS, pursuant to said Contract, Buyer deposited with the Seller's Broker as Earnest Money ("Earnest Money") the amount of $2,500.00, in the form of a personal check, deposited into the Seller's Broker's Trust Account which has not yet cleared the Seller's Broker's bank; and,

WHEREAS, there is a dispute between the parties and they wish to resolve their disputes as they relate to this contract and to forever fully release and discharge each other from any and all liability which may have arisen as a result of the indicated contract and the events that followed and provide for the disbursement of the Earnest Money;

NOW, THEREFORE, each of the parties hereby irrevocably covenants, promises and agrees as follows, with the knowledge and intent that the other parties rely on these promises, covenants, agreements and representations:

1. That the Earnest Money, as soon as the funds are considered collected funds, are available for withdrawal without limitation, and have cleared the banking system, be distributed as follows:

Seller $ _____   Buyer: $ _____

Seller's Agent: $ _____   Other Agent: $ _____

Other _____

2. Except with respect to the enforcement of this Mutual Release, the Parties, for themselves, their heirs, successors and assigns, do hereby remise, release and forever discharge each other, their representatives and agents,

servants, officers, directors, heirs, successors, and assigns, of and from any and all claims, actions, causes of action, demands, agreements, damages, costs, promises, expenses and compensation, in law or in equity, known or unknown, which the undersigned Parties, their respective, heirs, successors or assigns, or any of them, may have against one another or which may hereafter accrue or occur, in connection with, on account of, or in any way stemming from any transaction, matter, thing or occurrence the source of which is the Contract, including but not limited to, any and all claims of breach of any contract or agreement whether written or oral, any claims for money had and received, fraud, misrepresentation, negligence, breach of a fiduciary duty, specific performance, and any other claims based on any and all legal or equitable theories upon which a claim for relief or recovery can or could be based.

3. That the parties have each had an opportunity to seek legal counsel and have done so or elected not to do so as their sole and independent act and have not relied in any fashion on any representation made by any party or any agent or employee of any party for any advice or direction as to the advisability of entering into this Mutual Release.

4. That all parties understand that after this release is executed there will be no opportunity to reevaluate or reopen the matters herein indicated. It being the express purpose of this Mutual Release for everyone to forever completely release the other from any and all claims arising out of the Contract.

5. That in the event any party commences any legal action as a result of this release, whether to enforce it, defend an action based on it or otherwise, the nondefaulting party shall be entitled to a judgment in addition to all other sums, equal to the nondefaulting party's actual reasonable attorney's fees.

6. This Agreement may be executed in counterparts and, in that event, the counterparts, taken together, shall constitute a single instrument.

IN WITNESS WHEREOF, we the undersigned, after having fully read this agreement, hereby execute the same and receipt for a duplicate original of the same and for our respective checks in the amount indicated as being payable to each of us, on the day and date first above indicated.

Seller: Buyer:

_____   _____
Seller's Broker: Other Broker:
Denver Canadian Realty, Inc.

By: _____   _____

Earnest Money Dispute

DENVER CANADIAN
REALTY, INC.
420 Ponderosa Drive   Boulder, CO 80303
(303) 494-6661

Mr. and Mrs. Gary S. Joiner
4750 Table Mesa Drive
Boulder, CO 80303

Mr. and Mrs. Robert M. Cooper
Sunset Lodge Room 56A
Boulder, CO 80303

 Re: The Windhaven Property

Dear Mr. and Mrs. Joiner and Mr. and Mrs. Cooper:

 It is unfortunate that there has been an impasse as to the resolution of the earnest money deposit held by this company. There is currently on deposit in our trust account the sum of $ _____. According to Colorado law, we are prohibited from assessing the merits of competing claims to the earnest money or whether there is or is not a contract or a breach of contract. That is the job assigned to the court system, and we as real estate professionals are simply not licensed by this state to make that determination.

 We will hold the earnest money in our trustee or escrow account, segregated from our general operating funds, as provided by law, until either the court directs us as to how much to distribute and to whom or we receive the enclosed Mutual Release and Distribution Agreement signed by everyone.

 In the event that neither of those alternatives seems to be forthcoming, we will interplead the money into the District Court in this County, name each of you as having an interest in the funds, and ask the court to make a determination. You will note that your contract provides that we are entitled to recover our attorney's fees out of the earnest money in the event we are involved in any action dealing with the disposition of the earnest money. For that reason, we will endeavor to wait for what we feel is a reasonable time before taking any legal action to resolve the dispute.

Title Company Holds Earnest Money

 It is unfortunate that everyone cannot agree on the distribution of the earnest money deposit, currently in the amount of $500.00, held by Trautwein

Title and Abstract of Boulder, Inc. as escrow agent in their trust account. According to Colorado law, this firm and the title company are prohibited from determining the merits of competing claims to the earnest money or whether or not there is a valid contract dealing with the property or the earnest money or whether that contract has been breached. That is the job assigned to the court system, and we as real estate professionals are simply not licensed by this state to make that determination.

My conversations with the title company indicate that they will need a Mutual Release and Distribution Agreement executed by everyone before they will take any action to disburse the earnest money. A sample of their standard agreement is attached for your review. The title company has the option of interpleading the money into the District Court in this County, naming each of us as someone they feel may have an interest in the funds, and asking the court to make a determination. You will note that your contract provides that we are entitled to recover our attorney's fees out of the earnest money in the event we are involved in any action dealing with the disposition of the earnest money other than as claimants for our portion of the earnest money retained by the seller.

General Conclusion

I encourage you to seek competent legal counsel and decide amongst yourselves how you want to distribute the money. I am sorry that I cannot make this determination for us all; it is simply illegal for me to attempt a determination on the merits. I am a real estate broker and have no desire to be an attorney or a judge.

Thank you for your cooperation, understanding, and assistance in this matter. Please let me know if there is anything that I can do to assist either of you or your attorneys. Since we also have an attorney, we are sure that you will understand that we would like all communication to go through this office before our attorney is contacted so that we too can keep our attorney's fees from exceeding the earnest money.

Most sincerely,
Denver Canadian Realty, Inc.

Lee D. Weinstein

by: Lee D. Weinstein, Broker

cc: **ORIGINALS SENT CERTIFIED**
   Copies sent Regular Mail

Returning Earnest Money to a Trusted Client

Basic Considerations

There are those occasions when for whatever reasons, you decide to either deliver all or part of the earnest money to one of the parties. Sometimes it is apparent that one party does not intend to take any action or employ an attorney but is simply stalling and refusing to execute a release. Other times, for whatever reason, the amount in question simply does not lend itself to litigation. In small cases the exposure is very limited.

General Rule

As a general rule, I would never transfer the money to anyone other than my client. Cooperation, testimony, interest, and pressure are easier to control if you keep the money.

Broker Portion

You may be entitled to a portion of the forfeited earnest money. Retention of your portion may help to offset your potential loss and make the matter even less risky. Care should be exercised prior to distributing any money to a subagent as its recovery may be more difficult when the action starts. As a general rule, never pay anyone, especially subagents, buyers' brokers, or independent contractors until the matter is resolved. Obtaining a return of the money granted, no matter what agreement has been reached, will never be cost effective.

Notice

Prior to its distribution, it might be a good idea to put everyone on notice that you intend to distribute it and to specify the basis for your determination. The longer you have had the money, the greater the need to notify people. The failure to receive any formal or timely requests for its delivery does not eliminate the need to provide everyone with some form of notice. Certified Mail, Return Receipt Requested, Addressee Only, is obviously the best of the options.

Indemnification

There is no need to give anyone any money without an Indemnification Agreement holding the broker, agent, subagent, or other parties properly covered, harmless against any and all loss that the broker may sustain, including attorney's fees in the defense or ultimate payment of a claim to the money. The broker should reserve the right to settle any claim by paying the claim in full and receiving recovery from the seller. [Good Luck.] When you have had enough, you should be able to quit.

Collected Funds

I hate to tell you how many brokers, in a hurry to solve an earnest money problem, have written checks on uncollected funds. Be sure that the check that you received for the earnest money has cleared both your bank and the bank it was drawn on before you hand over the money. A good general rule is ten days, but make two simple phone calls and confirm it.

Aggressive Position—Earnest Money

DENVER CANADIAN
REALTY, INC.
420 Ponderosa Drive Boulder, CO 80303
(303) 494-6661

Mr. and Mrs. Gary S. Joiner
4750 Table Mesa Drive
Boulder, CO 80303

CERTIFIED MAIL

Mr. and Mrs. Robert M. Cooper
Sunset Lodge Room 56A
Boulder, CO 80303

    Re: The Windhaven Property
        Purchase and Sale Contract
        Dated December 23, 1955

Dear Mr. and Mrs. Joiner and Mr. and Mrs. Cooper:

This firm has been holding the earnest money in the amount of $500.00 for over a year since the transaction was supposed to close on January 28, 1976. This is a little amount of money and it does not seem appropriate for us to retain it indefinitely. Although we have the right to pay the money into the registry of the court and give you both the ability to enter your appearances and fight over the money, we have decided to take an alternate action.

After careful consideration and review of the matter with our attorneys, our feelings are as follows: The purchaser will never willingly allow the earnest money to be distributed under any terms to anyone; there is not enough money for anyone to hire an attorney and fight the matter; there has been no claim for the money in the form of litigation; the purchaser has never presented us with a substantiated claim to the money; therefore, feeling confident as we do with our relationship with the seller, and after receiving indemnification in a form acceptable to us from the seller, we are going to distribute the money to the seller. If, however, the buyers can, prior to noon on February 29th, 1988, present and substantiate their claim to the earnest money, specifically itemizing the facts that support the buyers' position in a manner that, in our opinion, is sufficient to warrant the money's continued retention, we will continue to retain the money.

Most sincerely,
Denver Canadian Realty, Inc.

Lee D. Weinstein

by: Lee D. Weinstein, Broker

cc: ORIGINALS SENT CERTIFIED
Copies sent Regular Mail

Chapter Six
Closing Matters

As closing approaches and passes, there are a lot of little items that will need your attention. This is a good time to patch up strained relationships, confirm forever the strong ones, and have a last stab at protecting yourself from the potential problems that lurk out there after closing. It is a nice time to reconfirm oral representations, attempt to bootstrap disclaimers that should have been made but were not and to try to make everyone feel that they will never have a claim against you in the future. Most litigation, with the exception of earnest money actions, comes after closing.

The Late Disclaimer

Closing is upon you and there are a few problems you would like to put to bed. Disclaimers, to be effective, must have taken place before the decision to purchase or sell was made. The theory is that the party had all the information, including the disclaimers, before he obligated himself on the contract. Once a party has changed his position, he will claim that had he known the facts you revealed in the disclaimer he would not have changed his position. In other words, he relied upon your silence or what he thought you indicated and you are now prevented from making an effective disclaimer since he cannot reverse the transaction, absent recession. Do not let that deter you. "Better late than never" definitely applies here. It is how the parties feel that is most important. If they feel that they have released you, that may be enough to remove an action against you from their minds.

Memorandum of Previous Oral Disclaimer

If you are put in the above position, I would suggest that you structure all disclaimers and other attempts to limit your liability in the form of memorandums of what was previously, timely, orally indicated to the proper party. Just start the statement with "This is a memorandum of our previous oral understanding" and then state whatever you feel you need.

Protective Language Placement at Closing

The best place to add in the necessary statements is directly on the closing statement. The front is nice and the back will do if necessary. Statements in your handwritting are not as good as typed ones and can raise some questions, but they are better than none at all. If you can get the person whom you are trying to protect yourself against to write it in their handwriting, you are doing very well indeed.

Hazard and Fire Insurance

This is all important. You will only have to have one fire while you are at closing, or one fire in the postclosing preoccupancy period, to become a devout insurance fanatic.

Regardless of the form of financing, always check for new insurance. Often in an assumption, the insurance is transferred to the new buyer. Care needs to be exercised to insure that there is in fact a policy in force and that, effective with the closing date, the buyer will be a named insured. There is no substitute for a written letter or endorsement from the company or the agent. It is an area very few people know anything about and a place for a disaster to occur and for you to be held responsible.

Case in Point

I will never forget sitting at the closing table when the call came in that the buyer's, my customer's, new home was on fire. I was in my rookie year and knew nothing about insurance. Fortunately, the buyer had obtained a paid insurance policy prior to attending the closing. The seller had forgotten to turn off a burner on the stove, and the buyer had put down a newspaper.

Nothing takes the place of a paid policy. Everything else is open for interpretation. Insurance companies make money collecting premiums, not paying claims. They know that.

Homeowner vs. Rental Policy

Different coverages exist for owner occupants and rental, or nonowner-occupied, property. If there is a change in the character, even for a few days, make sure the insurance reflects the actual use of the property. This loss is so rare that we tend to ignore the potential problem. It is so easy to provide for.

If the seller remains in possession of the property after the closing, he most probably has either canceled or transferred his policy to the purchaser, thereby not being covered since he is now a tenant. He is not insured and neither is his property. He needed a tenant's policy for this limited period.

Likewise, the buyer, not yet the occupant, may have obtained, either by assignment from the seller or independently, a homeowner's policy; although, he technically is not a homeowner occupant. His new insurance will not cover the loss of the possessions of the old owner occupant. He needed coverage similar to that of a landlord for this little period.

Inspection

If there is a provision for a preclosing inspection, it needs to be arranged in advance and a checklist approach followed. This is a good opportunity to avoid responsibility for items that were never your responsibility in the first place. Have the seller and purchaser check off the condition of the house as they go through it together.

A "standard" preclosing walk-through inspection sheet with "standard" wording printed at the bottom can be a useful tool. An item in the contract that indicates that the "buyer will be entitled to a walk-through prior to closing" but which, by implication, leaves open the options—other than total satisfaction—until the day of the walk-through can put you on in a tough position. There is often no mention of what will happen if the buyer disapproves of anything, major or minor, regarding the condition of the house. You may have created a monster. Use precise wording about walk-throughs. Do not let your deal walk through the floor. Here is an idea for the printed footer:

We have conducted a walk-through inspection of the property, and it is in the condition indicated on the contract, except as noted on this form. We understand that, excluding any attempt to conceal a defect known to the broker, the broker and his agents are not responsible for the condition of the property. We accept the property in the condition indicated on this form on this date.

Title Insurance

Some companies never issue the Title Insurance Policy. Without the actual policy, no one can make a claim. A tickler for about two weeks after closing can avoid latent problems. This also gives you the chance for additional contact with the purchaser and an opportunity to show how professional and detail-oriented you are.

Security

There is no excuse for failing to give a new buyer a written suggestion to get the property re-keyed immediately. Do not suggest anyone nor take this as a job that you will be responsible for arranging. It is simply a task for the buyer. So simply remind him.

Payment History

In the event that there is owner financing, the chances are good that no one will ever keep an accurate record of the payments made, the dates, the amounts, etc. Even new lenders make mistakes on occasion. The recommendation of a ledger system for both parties to track the payments serves two purposes. First, it gives them both the same form on which to make their entries. This alone will help simplify the problem when it arises. Second, for the life of the loan your name will be printed on the sample ledger card.

These items should be included as a minimum:

Date Paid   Check No   Amount Paid   Interest   Principal Balance

Document Retention

Few people have a grasp on the nature and value of important documents. Most people have not suffered a major casualty or loss by fire or theft. Advise the use of a safe deposit box for the Deed, the Title Insurance Policy, and especially for the owner-carry Note and Mortgage. If none is available, maybe you, under the right circumstances, could offer that service. It might be a nice way to keep in contact with the parties. Make sure you retain documents under a specific agreement.

DENVER CANADIAN
REALTY, INC.
420 Ponderosa Drive   Boulder, CO 80303
(303) 494-6661

Mr. and Mrs. Jon Goodman
420 Ponderosa Drive
Boulder, CO 80303

Mr. and Mrs. Gary S. Joiner
99 West Joggers Lane
Chicago, IL 99999

     Re: 420 Ponderosa Drive

Dear Mr. and Mrs. Goodman and Mr. and Mrs. Joiner:

     Congratulations on the purchase and sale of this nice property. All of us were glad to have been able to represent our seller and still assist the purchaser in this transaction. After closing there are a few administrative details that remain. Although we indicated them to each of you at the closing, we like to follow up with a letter to confirm what is yet to be done for both of your records. As you surely know by now, we are detail-oriented letter writers.

     The transaction provided for a loan to be carried by the seller for the purchaser. Since neither of you is in the lending business, we would suggest a little simple record-keeping procedure for you both. Of course, this is just our idea and your accountant or tax adviser may require different standards and records to be kept. Our suggestions are for the practical and not the legal or accounting record-keeping rules.

     Record on a ledger the following:

<u>Date Paid</u>   <u>Check No</u>   <u>Amount Paid</u>   <u>Interest</u>   <u>Principal Balance</u>

     In addition, save all checks and receipts that relate to the expenses related to the loan, the insurance, or the taxes and assessments. Gary and Karen, you need to keep the note and the deed of trust in a very safe place because they will be required for the ultimate payment and release of the loan.

     If we can assist you in any way, please do not hesitate to call.

               Most sincerely,
               Denver Canadian Realty, Inc.

               Lee D. Weinstein

               by: Lee D. Weinstein, Broker

Buyer—Title Policy and Deed

DENVER CANADIAN
REALTY, INC.
420 Ponderosa Drive   Boulder, CO 80303
(303) 494-6661

Mr. and Mrs. Jon Goodman
420 Ponderosa Drive
Boulder, CO 80303

    Re: 420 Ponderosa Drive

Dear Mr. and Mrs. Goodman:

    I am so glad that we could help you with the purchase of your new house. Although we represent many sellers, it is the satisfaction of a happy purchaser that allows us to work for our sellers properly. Nothing is as rewarding as knowing that I have been able to help a client sell a nice home to a family like yours. I know you will enjoy the home and I am glad that we have become friends.

    There are a couple of items that you need to watch for in the near future. First, after the deed has been recorded, it will be returned to your current address. If you do not get it in three weeks, please let me know. When it arrives, you should be prepared to put it in a safe place. The act of recording the deed evidences your acceptance of it and puts the world on notice that you own the property. A deed is not transferred by endorsement and therefore no one could obtain the physical deed and endorse it over to another purchaser in the way one might endorse a check. Still, I like to recommend that the deed be retained in a safe place.

    Similarly, the title policy will arrive in the mail in about four weeks. This is a different matter, and the actual policy needs to be retained in a safe place since it will have to be surrendered in the event of a problem or in the event that you want a reissue rate on a subsequent sale. If you do not receive this in the alloted time, contact me or the title company directly. It is very important that you obtain the policy and that you review it to insure that it reflects what the commitment promised.

    If you need someone to assist you in obtaining these documents, please let me know. There is no charge for this service, and I want to make sure the transaction is completed properly. I look forward to seeing you both as soon as you are settled in.

Sincerely,
Denver Canadian Realty, Inc.

Lee D. Weinstein

by: Lee D. Weinstein, Broker

Buyer—New Keys

DENVER CANADIAN
REALTY, INC.
420 Ponderosa Drive   Boulder, CO 80303
(303) 494-6661

Mr. and Mrs. Jon Goodman
420 Ponderosa Drive
Boulder, CO 80303

Re: 420 Ponderosa Drive

Dear Mr. and Mrs. Goodman:

Congratulations on your new home. I know you are excited to have completed the ordeal of finding it, contracting for it and financing it. Although we were the agents for the seller, we enjoyed assisting you in the transaction. You are the kind of people that we appreciate. Welcome home.

I know I mentioned it at closing, but I want to again remind you that although we knew the sellers very well, the key to your home has passed through many hands during the showing and sale procedure. We always recommend that new owners have the property re-keyed as soon as possible. We cannot be responsible for the integrity of the home or represent that you are the only people with keys.

[As I indicated to you at the closing, we cannot be responsible for the integrity of the property as the keys have been in many hands during the listing period. Our offer to pay for the re-keying of the home by an agent of your selection is still open. Just tell us the amount of the bill and we will either pay them directly or reimburse you for the expense.]

Thank you for selecting this office to assist you in locating your new house. I am glad that we have met. I hope your son is enjoying the swing set and the tree house. Both Nancy and I hope to see you at the pool this summer.

Sincerely,
Denver Canadian Realty, Inc.

Lee D. Weinstein

by: Lee D. Weinstein, Broker

Chapter Seven

The Rest of
the World

Third Party Letters

Telephone Trust

The telephone is used to such an extent that we never even know with whom we speak or how to verify the information or quotes that we rely upon. Lenders, title companies, inspection services, surveyors, taxing authorities, homeowners' associations, ditch and water companies, municipal and other governmental and quasi-governmental authorities and similar entities provide us with information that we accept, pass on to our clients and customers and fail to verify or commit to memory. Too often the information changes and the memory of the person we have spoken with and relied upon, now to our detriment, fades as time and pressure are applied.

Silent Response

The silent response cover letter is a useful tool to establish a duty on the part of the recipient to either respond or accept the consequences, and, although not as good as the required response cover letter, it is far better than no letter at all. Coupled with a log of conversations, incorporating the name of the party you are talking with as well as the date, time and content of the conversation, plus the limited use of certified mail, the silent response letter can put you in a very defensible position. It not only documents the content of the conversation but also demonstrates the degree of care utilized to bring the information to the client or customer.

Copies

Copies, policy, and habit are the added plums that give your testimony the credibility that is needed to place the burden of proof on the person who failed to respond. Never let yourself get caught in the position of not responding if such a tactic is used on you. Many people simply do not want to respond if they know the answer is not what they have indicated over the phone or that it will cause the recipient to question the response. People simply try to do what they like to do and leave the unpleasant work for later. This is sudden death when you are utilizing the silent response letter arrangement.

Buyer's Brokers and Subagents

Confirming the relationship between your office and that of the other broker is a good way to avoid future misunderstandings, keep good friends as good friends, and avoid ethics and arbitration problems. A blanket letter or a specific letter will highlight your concerns and agreements.

DENVER CANADIAN
REALTY, INC.
420 Ponderosa Drive   Boulder, CO 80303
(303) 494-6661

Mr. Ed Schmale, Broker
Pacific United Realty
21 North Center Green
Denver, CO 80213

    Re: Subagency Relationship
          Smith Road Property
          Hampden and Fifth Streets

Dear Ed:

    Thank you for calling this office to inquire about acting as our subagents with regard to the above property. We are offering a commission equal to ____% of the total sales price of the property to the successful subagent who procures the purchaser ready, willing and able to complete the transaction as proposed by the seller, our principal. This obligation to pay you such a commission and the payment of commission itself are subject to the following terms and conditions:

    First, you are the agent who procures the purchaser that ultimately purchases the property. To insure that there is no confusion, the names of all prospective purchasers must be submitted to this office, either before you show the property or within twenty-four hours after the scheduled showing. We intend to give those names to the seller, our client, in order to provide protection for both of us in the event that a purchaser should try to circumvent our listing agreement.

    Second, our obligation to pay a commission is predicated upon our receipt of the same in cash. Should we be forced to accept conditional payment, which we may in our sole discretion elect to do, we will not be obligated to pay you until we are paid. In addition, we shall have no obligation to institute any form of collection procedure, including litigation, to collect the commission due. Should such action be necessary, you will be expected to share, in advance and on demand, in the expense of collection, including attorney's fees for the attorney I select, or forfeit your right to any portion of the proceeds of such an effort.

Third, that you do not compromise the interests of the seller, our principal, by your actions or inactions. We require that you provide us, in a timely fashion, with any information that you possess as to the financial qualifications of the purchaser, his intentions, and the amount that he will ultimately be willing to offer for the property. We understand that you will use your best efforts on behalf of the seller to obtain the highest and best offer possible.

Your acceptance of this proposal is evidenced by your taking any action with regard to the real estate without first giving us a written statement to indicate that you are not accepting the proposal. You will be responsible for your own actions and inactions not consistent with the laws of agency in this state and the terms of this letter.

It is a pleasure to have you as a subagent for the potential sale of this property. Please understand that this commission split is not offered with the intention that you split any listing commissions which you may independently have originated and upon which we become your subagents in the same fashion.

Most sincerely,
Denver Canadian Realty, Inc.

Lee D. Weinstein

by: Lee D. Weinstein, Broker

DENVER CANADIAN
REALTY, INC.
420 Ponderosa Drive   Boulder, CO 80303
(303) 494-6661

Ms. Sharon Reichman, Broker
Pacific United Realty
21 North Center Green
Denver, CO 80303

  Re: Subagency Relationship
    General Terms

Dear Sharon:

  Thank you for you inquiry. This letter is to confirm the extent of and terms upon which you may act as our subagents for property that we have listed. Subject to the terms and conditions of this letter, we will pay you a commission equal to ___% of the total sales price of any property that is sold and closed with a purchaser that you procure, such procurement, of course, being within our listing period and any proper extensions or protection periods that may exist thereunder. This obligation to pay you such a commission and the payment of commission itself are subject to the following terms and conditions:

  First, you are the agent who procures the purchaser that ultimately purchases the property. To insure that there is no confusion, the names of all prospective purchasers must be submitted to this office, either before you show the property or within twenty four hours after the scheduled showing. We intend to give those names to the seller, our client, in order to provide protection for both of us in the event that a purchaser should try to circumvent our listing agreement.

  Second, our obligation to pay a commission is predicated upon our receipt of the same in cash. Should we be forced to accept conditional payment, which we may in our sole discretion elect to do, we will not be obligated to pay you until we are paid. In addition, we shall have no obligation to institute any form of collection procedure, including litigation, to collect the commission due. Should such action be necessary, you will be expected to share, in advance and on demand, in the expense of collection, including attorney's fees for the attorney I select, or forfeit your right to any portion of the proceeds of such an effort.

Third, that you do not compromise the interests of the seller, our principal, by your actions or inactions. We require that you provide us, in a timely fashion, with any information that you possess as to the financial qualifications of the purchaser, his intentions, and the amount that he will ultimately be willing to offer for the property. We understand that you will use your best efforts on behalf of the seller to obtain the highest and best offer possible.

Fourth, except with regard to parties that are disclosed to us as herein provided, this agreement may be cancelled by this office at will, and in no event, unless extended in writing, shall it remain in effect after midnight on the 12th of March, 1999.

Your acceptance of this proposal is evidenced by your returning an executed copy of this agreement to this office on or before noon on the 12th of March, 1987. Absent such acceptance we shall assume that any action or inquiry taken with regard to any property in which this office has an interest, as agent or as owner, is in the capacity of an agent for a prospective purchaser without compensation from this office.

Anticipating that you will accept, let me tell you that we are glad to have you as a competitor and potential subagent. Please sell all the property that you can that is listed with this office. You will, of course, be responsible for your own actions and inactions not consistent with the laws of agency in this state and the terms of this letter. We both understand that we are free to make the same, similar, and different agreements with other potential subagents without regard to the contents of this agreement upon such terms and conditions that we alone determine are adequate without regard for or notification to you.

Please understand that this is not a proposal for a reciprocal agreement, and no such agreement is sought by this letter. In the event you wish to discuss the terms under which you will allow us to act as your subagents, please let me know. You are under no obligation to pay us upon the same terms or conditions that are agreed upon here for your payment.

Most sincerely,
Denver Canadian Realty, Inc.

Lee D. Weinstein

by: Lee D. Weinstein, Broker

Mr. LaVerne Davis
SanVern Realty Consultants
Boulder, CO 80303

    Re: Buyer's Brokerage Arrangement

Dear LaVerne:

    Thank you for your inquiry regarding our policy for dealing with potential buyers' brokers or agents of the purchaser. As you know, we are very interested in marketing our seller's property to all interested buyers. We welcome the participation of buyers' brokers and, subject to the qualifications outlined in this letter, are willing to acknowledge your agency relationship with your buyers.

    1. That upon your initial contact, you advise our office of the fact that you are acting as a buyer's agent for the potential sale of the particular property indicated and of the compensation agreement that exists with your principal. This need not include the amount that you are going to be paid by your principal but must indicate one of the following methods of payment:

        a. In the event you are to be compensated in whole or in part from the buyer, we will not agree to pay any portion of your commission.

        b. In the alternative, we will agree to pay you a commission, pursuant to the terms herein expressed equal to the greater of ___% of the ultimate selling price or the amount that is being offered for potential subagents.

    Upon initial contact we do not need to know the name of your buyer; however, you agree to provide us with that name immediately upon request should we need to disclose it to our seller to protect our rights to receive a commission.

    2. You are the agent who procures the purchaser that ultimately purchases the property. This is determined by the inclusion of your name on the offer

that is provided to this office. We reserve the right to include you in, or exclude you from, the presentation of any offer or other negotiations with the seller.

3. Our obligation to pay a commission is predicated upon our receipt of the same in cash. Should we be forced to accept conditional payment, which we may in our sole discretion elect to do, we will not be obligated to pay you until we are paid. In addition, we shall have no obligation to institute any form of collection procedure, including litigation to collect the commission due. Should such action be necessary, you will be expected to share, in advance and on demand, in the expense of collection, including attorney's fees for the attorney I select, or forfeit your right to any portion of the proceeds of such an effort. We reserve the right to require, as a condition precedent to payment, a statement from your principal outlining the fact that you are not receiving anything of value from that principal as a result of this transaction, i.e., that you are not also being paid by the purchaser.

4. This agreement may be canceled or modified by this office at any time unilaterally, except that such cancellation or modification shall not effect any transaction or buyer disclosure that is in effect on the date of cancellation or modification. This agreement shall, except as above provided, terminate at midnight on the 12th of March, 1999.

5. On a case-by-case basis, we reserve the right to indicate on your initial contact any of the following conditions: that this property is not covered by this agreement and that your agency status will not be acknowledged, or that we cannot compensate you for your efforts. To be effective, we will indicate this to you on your initial contact and confirm such an exception to this agreement in a letter of even date. We are sorry that this is a possibility; however, the different aspects of various listings may prohibit us from accepting a buyer's agency or from taking on the obligation to compensate buyers' agents.

Your acceptance of this proposal is evidenced by your returning an executed copy of this agreement to this office on or before noon on the 12th of March, 1987. [Your acceptance is evidenced by your indicating your agency status when calling this office in the future and obtaining information about a listing.] Absent such acceptance, we shall assume that any action or inquiry taken with regard to any property in which this office has an interest, as agent or as owner, is in the capacity of an agent for a prospective purchaser without compensation from this office.

We are happy to have you as a competitor and to provide you with access to the properties that we have listed. We expect you to exercise due care and to safeguard the property and possessions of the sellers we represent at all times. Please sell all the property that you can that is listed with this office. You will, of course, be responsible for your own actions and inactions not consistent with the laws of agency in this state and the terms of this letter. We both understand that we are free to make the same, similar, and different agreements with other potential buyers' brokers and subagents without regard to the contents of this agreement upon such terms and conditions that we alone determine are adequate without any obligation to notify you.

Please understand that this is not a proposal for a reciprocal agreement, and no such agreement is sought by this letter. In the event you wish to discuss the terms under which you will allow us to act as your subagents or buyers' brokers for the sale of your listings, please let me know. You are under no obligation to pay us upon the same terms or conditions that are agreed upon here for your payment.

Most sincerely,
Denver Canadian Realty, Inc.

Lee D. Weinstein

by: Lee D. Weinstein, Broker

DENVER CANADIAN
REALTY, INC.
420 Ponderosa Drive   Boulder, CO 80303
(303) 494-6661

Ms. Rosie Habrock
Westwind Mortgage, Inc.
1900 West Chambers Drive
Phoenix, AZ 99900

Re: Jon Goodman—Loan Quote

Dear Rosie:

Thank you for taking the time to give me an oral quote yesterday for current VA and FHA loans. With the market as hectic as it appears, I know you have a lot to do and I appreciate your stopping to help me. I have passed the information you gave me along to Jon Goodman and his wife, as they prepare to write a contract on 1568 Bellaire Drive, and just want to make a little note so that I will remember the specifics of the quote.

Understanding of course that any quote presupposes that the borrower can meet the VA or FHA qualification guidelines, and that there are funds authorized by the Congress of the United States to fill the loan, please review my understandings and let me know by express return mail or Federal Express if I have made an error.

The quote is for a maximum FHA loan, or such loan as the Goodmans are approved for, with a fixed interest rate of 10% per annum, providing for equal monthly payments amortized over 30 years, with a 1% origination fee and 4.5% discount points being the total points or percentage fees based on the loan amount that will be due at the closing of the loan.

This commitment is open for a sixty-day period from our conversation, which means that if the Goodmans apply within the next week for the loan and it is approved within the sixty-day period, they may elect to take advantage of this committed rate, these terms and points, and you will honor the above commitment, regardless of the market conditions at that time.

This commitment is a floating commitment and does not bind you to make the loan at this rate and terms, the Goodmans being free to apply for and await approval of their loan, committing at any time during this procedure and even after the loan is approved for the rate and points that are quoted on the date they elect to commit. Thereafter, so long as the loan is scheduled to close, and there is no delay on the part of the Goodmans, the indicated rate, terms and points will remain a fixed commitment on your part.

In either event, the 1% loan origination fee will be payable when the rate is locked in as a nonrefundable fee, which will apply to the total of the origination and discount points quoted.

Since this is a conventional loan I understand that, depending on the loan-to-value ratio, you may require private mortgage insurance (PMI). If this is the case, the loan will have to be approved not only by your loan committee but also by your PMI underwriter, which you think usually takes an extra three days. Their fees, collected by you, are in addition to the fees indicated and are 1/2% additional origination fee, 1% additional discount points and will increase the loan rate by 1/4% per annum to a total rate of 10.25% per annum. These fees will not be required as long as the loan amount is equal to or less than 70% of the appraised value as determined by an appraiser utilized by your company.

If I have made an error please call me at the above telephone number and follow that call up with a letter sent either certified mail or federal express or express mail as I want to be sure that I inform the Goodmans accurately of your rate quote. I hope their contract is accepted and that they select you for the new loan because I know you can get the processing done on time in a professional manner and get the loan closed. You know I enjoy working with you and your company and look forward to another successful contract, loan and closing.

Most sincerely,
Denver Canadian Realty, Inc.

James C. Smittkamp

by: James C. Smittkamp, Sales Agent

cc: Jon Goodman, Buyer

Other Broker—Loan Approval

DENVER CANADIAN
REALTY, INC.
420 Ponderosa Drive   Boulder, CO 80303
(303) 494-6661

Mrs. Sandy Miller
SanVern Realty and Investment
Boulder, CO. 80303

Re: 1910 Stony Hill Road

Dear Sandy:

Thank you for the news that the loan requested by the buyers was approved by Richmond Mortgage yesterday. I knew Tom Richmond would be able to help them determine the best financing and process the application to a commitment. I know you have conveyed the news to the buyers. I have told the seller the good news. It is also nice to have the commitment before the deadline in the contract.

Thank you for your efforts. My records indicate that the title commitment was delivered to your office on the 13th, and I understand that you gave it to the buyers the same day. That is another deadline that was properly met.

There are still a few items to be completed and I wanted to outline them here so that we may each know the extent of our tasks.

[Indicate who will do what and by when.]

I look forward to another smooth closing on the 15th, at 2:00 P.M., at the title company offices. It has been nice to have you as the buyer's agent on this particular transaction. I enjoy working with you. Please let me know if there is anything that either I or the seller can do to assist you in your transition.

Most sincerely,
Denver Canadian Realty, Inc.

Lee D. Weinstein

by: Lee D. Weinstein, Broker

cc: Gary S. Joiner, Seller
[Copies to your clients or customers of third party letters serve to inform your client or customer of the progress being made and make them aware of the content of the letter as efficiently as if the letters had been addressed to them.]

Mr. Tom Richmond
Richmond and Company Mortgage, Inc.
125 West Heavenly Drive
Boulder, CO 80303

    Re: 56894 East Happy Canyon Lane
       George Kellermain and Sandy Smith

Dear Betty:

    I was so happy to get your call today indicating that the loan to these borrowers on their new home has been approved. Thank you for taking the time to call. As you know, the loan condition was to run out today and they would have had to elect to deposit additional earnest money, forfeit their existing earnest money, or allow the seller to take the backup offer. Your call came just in time.

    I have told my customers that your approval was on the terms listed below. Please take a minute to check my understanding and let me know by telephone and certified mail if this is not the case.

1. Loan Amount $125,000.00
2. Fixed interest rate of 10.5% per annum
3. Thirty-year term with a ten-year call
4. Loan origination fee of 1%
5. Loan Discount Fees of 3.5%
6. Loan closing date of July 4, 1990
7. Loan commitment good through August 15, 1990

    I knew you could get this loan approved and I appreciate the opportunity to be involved with a loan that you are handling. I know that you were of great assistance in helping George and Sandy review their finances and in selecting this particular loan as the best one for their needs. Good loan counselors such as you are hard to find. I look forward to seeing you at closing.

> Most sincerely,
> Denver Canadian Realty, Inc.
>
> *James C. Smittkamp*
>
> by: Jim Smittkamp, Agent

cc: Gary and Karen Joiner

DENVER CANADIAN
REALTY, INC.
420 Ponderosa Drive   Boulder, CO 80303
(303) 494-6661

Mr. Jon Goodman and
Mrs. Mimi Goodman
Room 24 Lookout Motel and Casino
Grand Forks, WA 99876

     Re: 64 Westview Lane

Dear Jon and Mimi:

This letter has good news and I am glad to bring it to you. Enclosed is a copy of the letter I just sent to Rosie at Westwind Mortgage confirming my conversation with her today wherein she indicated that your loan has been approved on the terms you requested. [This is the day we have been waiting for; the loan you selected has been approved.]

I never really believe it until the mortgage company actually writes the check, but I have scheduled the closing for the date indicated in the contract, July 16th, 1989, at the offices of Westwind Mortgage in Oakbrook. I will be contacting you as soon as I have the exact figures so that we can arrange for the actual closing time and I can provide you with directions to their office.

Just a last reminder, please review the title insurance commitment that I dropped off at Jon's office yesterday. Just call Cindy, Pam or Jennifer at the title company, 449-7500. They are ready to answer any questions that you may have. If I do not hear to the contrary, I will assume that the document meets with your approval.

There are only a few items left on the checklist to be completed. Remember, you need to:

1. Contact Public Service, 623-1234, to arrange for the power to be turned on.

2. Make your final inspection on Friday at 3:00 P.M.; I will be picking you both up at the motel at 2:45.

If there is anything else that I can do, please do not hesitate to call me immediately. Looks like you are on the way into your new home. Congratulations.

Most sincerely,
Denver Canadian Realty, Inc.

Lee D. Weinstein

by: Lee D. Weinstein, Broker

DENVER CANADIAN
REALTY, INC.
420 Ponderosa Drive   Boulder, CO 80303
(303) 494-6661

Ms. Rosie R. Habrock
Westwind Mortgage, Inc.
1900 West Chambers Drive
Phoenix, AZ 99900

     Re: Charles A. Reasoner's Application

Dear Betty:

    I hope all is going well with this loan application. The approval deadline still is August 5th, and I know there are other contracts just waiting for this one to collapse so please let me know if there is anything else that I can do to help you. The proper, timely completion of this loan application and the closing of the contract are the most important things to me.

    Here is the copy of the Planned Unit Development that I picked up from Mr. J.R. Easygoing, the Manager of the City Housing Authority. I do not know how they find anything down there so I just asked for the "PUD on Westhaven in Oakridge" and this is what he gave me. If it is not what you need please let me know today.

    Again, I want to thank you for working with the Reasoners and helping them with their selection of their loan program. I know how to sell real estate and like leaving the selection of the proper and adequate financing to you and the buyers privately. I know they value your professional assistance.

                    Most sincerely,
                    Denver Canadian Realty, Inc.

                    Lee D. Weinstein

                    by: Lee D. Weinstein, Broker

cc: Charles A. Reasoner, Buyer

Ms. Cindy Trautwein
Trautwein Title and Abstract Company
1600 Fairview Lane
Boulder, CO 80303

    Re: Commitment Number 56-89234-890

Dear Cindy:

    Thank you for moving fast to obtain the title insurance commitment for this transaction. I appreciate your delivering a copy of it to the Reasoners at their motel room at the Best Western Boulder Inn, as well as the copy that you left at this office. As usual I have told the Reasoners that you are the person to talk with if they have any questions about the specifics of the commitment.

    I did not see in the copy of the commitment delivered to my office the indication that you were going to provide Form 130 coverage, assuming that you get the survey and your standard lien waiver signed at closing. Please remember that all my transactions have that as a requirement, unless I indicate to the contrary. If you would send that endorsement to everyone today, I would really appreciate it.

    As you know, I like copies of all documents that relate to any typed exceptions and any covenants and restrictions that effect the property attached to each copy of the commitment. The copy of the commitment I received did not contain all of the covenants and restrictions and I fear that the buyer's copy may also have been short. If you would include a full set of the indicated copies with the Form 130 endorsement, it would save an additional trip.

    Please excuse my nagging, I am a detail-oriented person who must know that the parties have all the information they require to arrive at their own decisions. I know that we both want a perfect closing and an informed buyer. I have indicated to the buyers that as long as we close in your office, you will update the commitment to the latest possible date and provide gap protection for any items that do not appear on the commitment or the update which goes of record prior to the recording of the deed. Although I am sure that the buyers desire this coverage, I am ordering it in my own right if necessary to insure that it is in effect. [The buyers want to be sure that that coverage is obtained.] I have assured the buyers that you will take care of obtaining the endorsement and gap protection.

You have my standard closing instruction sheet and I would appreciate it if you would deliver a set of the closing papers to both attorneys indicated thereon at least three days prior to the closing for their review. Again, it is nice to deal with such a professional title company, but it is you who make the transaction close properly and I am proud to be able to send you this additional business. If there is anything that I can do to expedite this transaction, please let me know right away.

Most sincerely,
Denver Canadian Realty, Inc.

Lee D. Weinstein

by: Lee D. Weinstein, Broker

cc: Charles A. Reasoner

Builder Contracts

Standard Form Contracts

The requirements concerning the drafting and use and of "standard" or "approved" forms, and the completion of the same vary widely from state to state. Real estate licensees in many states are allowed only to fill in the blanks and thereby complete a state-approved form. In some states, attorneys are the only ones who can complete real estate contracts. However, the parties may select and complete forms to their hearts' content.

The Standard Builder Contract

Many builders, feeling for whatever reason that the forms offered by whatever agency of the government, a board or the bar association, are not as they would wish them, have developed a specific form for the use of all agents working through their listing broker. Although there is no prohibition indicating that a prospective purchaser cannot utilize any form that strikes his fancy, these sellers are so heavily regulated and concerned about litigation that they will generally insist that all offers be on their form. Only the pressure of the market can alter this firm stance. The broker needs to make his agents and subagents aware of the seller's requirements and at the same time indicate to all concerned that the broker is not responsible for the contents of or omissions in this or any other form.

DENVER CANADIAN
REALTY, INC.
420 Ponderosa Drive   Boulder, CO 80303
(303) 494-6661

Mr. Lawrence S. Schreder, President
Central Colorado Construction Company, Inc.
4th and Main Street
Colorado Springs, CO 80903

     Re: Standard Form Contracts

Dear Larry:

     I am happy to have the listing on the existing and "to-be-built" homes in your Applewood subdivision in the Lake of the Never-Ending Trail. I know that you understand that I need to write this letter to confirm what we have discussed in the past regarding your instructions for the use of the standard form contract that you have provided our office.

     Let me congratulate you on your efforts to select and draft a contract especially for your sales, instead of using the standard real estate commission-approved form. As you know, I am a real estate broker and not an attorney, and, therefore, I could not help with the drafting effort. It is nice to have legal counsel to write contracts so that all we have to do is fill in the blanks.

     Neither Denver Canadian Realty, Inc., I, nor any of my agents can possibly be responsible for the content of the contract. We will, however, complete it according to your direction. In addition, as you have indicated, we have been telling and continue to tell all potential buyers and subagents that all offers must be on your form. This may not stop someone from trying another form of an offer but it should discourage all but a few. No matter what form is utilized by a buyer, however, we will present it to you for your consideration.

                 Sincerely,
                 Denver Canadian Realty, Inc.

Lee D. Weinstein

                 by: Lee D. Weinstein, Broker

Subagent's Use of Special Form

DENVER CANADIAN
REALTY, INC.
420 Ponderosa Drive   Boulder, CO 80303
(303) 494-6661

Mr. John Roberts, Broker
Roberts and Company Real Estate
789 Westhaven Drive
Boulder, CO 80303

Re: Never-Ending Trail

Dear John:

This will confirm that our office, as the listing agent for Central Colorado Construction Company, Inc., has been instructed to utilize the contract form provided by our principal for the sales of properties in this development. I have enclosed copies of the desired form so that you will have them available for any sales you may make in this area.

Understand that this office is not responsible for the content of this contract. Should you need assistance in its completion, please do no hesitate to ask for a sample of a completed contract. I think that the seller has obtained this contract from his attorney and will not consider the use of other forms. However, I will be happy to present any offer that one of your customers may request.

Finally, regardless of any other arrangement that we may have with regard to co-op fees on other properties, your office will receive a co-op fee equal to ___% of the total sales price, including extras, upon the actual closing and receipt of the purchase price by the seller. In the event of a dispute between this office and the seller, we reserve the right to settle that dispute in any fashion that we deem appropriate, including waiving our collective right to a commission and co-op split entirely. Should there be a reduction in the gross commission, we will share such a reduction equally. Your showing of any property in the development will constitute your acceptance, not only of our offer of subagency but also of the terms of payment indicated herein. It is our position that once you are a subagent for any property in this development, you cannot become or act in the capacity of an agent for any potential buyer.

Sincerely,
Denver Canadian Realty, Inc.

Lee D. Weinstein

by: Lee D. Weinstein, Broker

Sample Closing Lines

The Final Words

When you finish a letter, keep in mind the many ways to end it. The following are some sample closing lines. They vary from the simple to the firm and almost offensive. The last thing you say should be congratulatory, polite, and nice. Always end correspondence with something that is not controversial. Use these separately or combine as needed. Add your own favorites.

Examples

Please forgive the formality of this letter. It is important for me to document, for everyone concerned, what information [advice is not a good word to use unless you mean it and are willing to stand by it] I have given you and the decisions that you have made. It may seem fastidious, but it is our office policy and helps keep my broker, the Real Estate Commission, and our malpractice carrier happy.

It is my understanding that you completely understand the transaction outlined by both this letter and our previous correspondence; and, after considering all the alternatives plus the potential risks involved, you have elected to proceed along the course outlined herein.

The transaction which you contemplate and which has been outlined in this letter is one that has serious tax, financial, and legal consequences. Please understand that neither I nor anyone associated with this office is recommending that you complete the transaction in the manner you have elected. We simply are not responsible for anything that occurs as a result of your decision.

Again, I would advise you to seek competent legal, accounting, and tax advice before entering into this transaction as you have outlined it.

As I indicated to you earlier, the decision to propose the terms you have proposed in the contract and the decision to acquire the property indicated above are your decisons alone. I must send you this letter to verify that you are acting on your own judgment and without any encouragement from or advice from me or this office. I know you want to complete the transaction as you have outlined it and I wish you the best of luck.

The property is simply beautiful and I know both you and Margaret will enjoy living in the Meadows. If we can be of service in assisting you in the locating other property in the future, please do not hesitate to inquire.

I have enjoyed showing you property and admire your ability to make your own decisions.

Congratulations on your acquisition of another piece of real estate. I wish you the best of luck and thank you for selecting me and this firm to show you property.

I admire your grasp of the complex issues presented and the business risks involved. Congratulations upon your decision to propose and complete this transaction as you have outlined.

As I have indicated to you all along, and as I know you understand, I have to write you a letter confirming the fact that you and you alone have decided to propose and complete this transaction and that neither I nor the office I work for nor the broker for the office can be in any way responsible for the outcome of the transaction. I admire your drive and grasp of the issues and wish you the best of luck.

Appendix

This appendix includes the most requested forms from the live presentations (people wanted them in the book) and also passes along some new ideas, those that have occurred to me and those that have evolved from ideas participants have discussed at my seminars.

When the first edition of this book was printed I thought it would be a resource for my clients. I never dreamed it would become not only a popular handbook utilized by many real estate professionals but also the basis for continuing education credit courses that taught risk reduction and management as well as marketing success. The live presentation is now available on audio and video cassette. The forms and sample letters in the book have been made available electronically on magnetic media for IBM and compatibles, as well as for Macintosh computers with a word processing program.

With the book as the basic reference and with the training tapes available, the entire risk reduction system is ready for immediate implementation throughout your office without the need to retype most of the material.

Disclosure Forms

Formal Notice of Closing and Settlement

This form was designed to encourage recalcitrant individuals to complete what they had already agreed to do in the first place: close the transaction. Written in a state that has face-to-face closing, it has been adapted from the form that appears here for the states that use escrow closing. I designed and have used the form for the purpose indicated with great success over the years and wanted to pass along the idea to everyone. I always indicate, however, to the prospective client that the attempt to compel someone to attending the closing or closing of escrow will "probably fail" so as not to raise the expectations of the client in advance and therefore precipitate a future problem if the notice does in fact not work. With few exceptions, it works very well.

This sample form is used as an example in the live presentation to demonstrate the effects that paper or "legal paper" can have upon all of us. How are we influenced by a form or a "standard" form, type of paper, size of type, use of bold characters, use of white space, redline margins, signatures, a notary seal, the color of ink, and finally the delivery of the document? Many people use these factors to determine the importance that they will place on the message they have just received.

This form should not be utilized without obtaining the approval of your attorney. Although I have indicated that the form is a "Standard Approved Form" and given it a form number, this is simply to emphasize how such notification gives an otherwise innocuous document an added degree of credibility. It never ceases to amaze me how influenced I am by a "standard" form. This version is on letter length paper to fit in this book. I would suggest redline, legal length (14 inch) bond paper for your use.

Once completed and served on the recalcitrant party, preferably less than 12 hours before the closing, I have found that the mere contact with the legal system is enough to give otherwise cold buyers or sellers the nudge to complete the transaction. Do not underrate the effect of having this form served by the local sheriff. While there is no legal significance to the person who serves a document, there is a psychological difference that cannot be overstated. The sheriff with his distinctive vehicle and uniform gives impact to the delivery of any document.

Good luck and use caution. Modify this form to suit your particular needs. No, it will not work if the buyer or seller do not have the money or the loan or loan assumption is not approved.

Seller's Property Disclosure

Many states and companies have already acquired and are presently utilizing some type of a property disclosure form. It is essential that the seller is the one who makes the representation, completes the property disclosure form, and insists that it be delivered to a prospective purchaser before the purchaser makes an offer to purchase. In addition, many states and companies are in the process of adopting, recommending or even requiring the use of such a form. This sample form, promulgated and approved by the Colorado Real Estate Commission is standard in Colorado. It represents a "place to start" to be utilized by those who do not yet have access to a state-approved or company-promulgated form. By no means an endall, it is presented for your consideration only.

Such a form is best utilized and most effective if it is given to the prospective purchaser before the purchaser drafts the initial contract (offer) to purchase the property. Failure to include it as a part of the initial offer will require a counteroffer, legally a rejection of the purchaser's offer, and a counterproposal. That then would require the written acceptance and approval of the seller to be a binding contract. Since the purchaser could refuse to sign and thereby "get out of the transaction," it might be the thing that killed an otherwise sold transaction. I recommend that it be an exhibit to the initial offer.

The question is, "How do we get it to a prospective buyer?" One answer, utilized by an increasing number of liability conscious brokers is to leave an ample supply of copies of the form as signed by the seller (I prefer it to be filled in by the seller in the seller's own handwriting to avoid the obvious allegations of alteration) in a little box (cardboard, plastic, wood, brass or gold as each particular listing and your budget may require or deserve) inside each listed property. The box could have a label that clearly states:

PLEASE TAKE ONE
MUST BE ATTACHED TO EVERY OFFER

In addition, a copy of the blowup of the MLS sheet could be stapled to each such Seller's Property Disclosure Form. I would discourage the use of life-size pictures and other marketing material picturing the listing broker or attempting to sell the listing broker to those prospective purchasers that are viewing the home. That discourages the needed cooperation of the subagent or buyer broker showing the property. We want to get the property sold for our client, the seller.

FORMAL NOTICE
OF
CONTRACT CLOSING AND SETTLEMENT

YOU ARE HEREBY FORMALLY INFORMED that on the day and date below indicated, the indicated closing agent will, after preparing all the required legal documents and calculating the amounts due and payable, be present, pursuant to the terms of the contract for the purchase and sale of real property indicated herein, to conduct the closing of that certain contract dated _____, 19____, entered into by and between: _____

_____ as purchaser(s)

and _____, as seller(s) for the purchase and sale of the following described real property, towit:

CLOSING AGENT/LOCATION:

      CLOSING DATE: _____, 19_____.

      CLOSING TIME: _____:_____ (a.m.) (p.m.)

WHEN AND WHERE YOU MAY APPEAR prepared to close according to the terms of said contract.

FAILURE TO APPEAR may subject you, the defaulting party, to the following legal action indicated in said contract:

FUNDS REQUIRED: The Purchaser and/or Seller must present a cashier's check or certified check drawn upon a local clearing house bank payable to the order of the indicated closing agent, or cash in the final settlement amount herein below indicated. The basis for, and the calculation of, said amount shall be made available to all parties for inspection at the date, place and time of closing.

SELLER: $_____.____   PURCHASER: $_____.____

IN WITNESS WHEREOF, AFTER BEING DULY SWORN UPON OATH, the undersigned has executed this Formal Notice of Contract Closing and Settlement this _____ day of _____, 19_____

SELLER: _____

by: _____ , authorized agent and attorney

WITNESS MY HAND AND OFFICIAL SEAL this _____ day of _____ 19_____

Seller, by _____

_____

    Clerk of the Court or Notary Public

My commission expires: _____

Standard Approved Form # 82-9802
© 1990 Real Law Books, Inc. P.O.Box 3113 Boulder, CO 80307 All Rights Reserved (303)494-4661

The printed portions of this form approved by the
Colorado Real Estate Commission

**THIS DISCLOSURE SHOULD BE
COMPLETED BY THE SELLER**

SELLER'S PROPERTY DISCLOSURE

Date: _____

Seller states that the information contained in this Disclosure is correct to the best of Seller's **CURRENT ACTUAL KNOWLEDGE** as of the above date. Broker may deliver a copy of this Disclosure to prospective purchasers.

PROPERTY ADDRESS _____

1. THE FOLLOWING ARE IN THE CONDITIONS INDICATED:

a. APPLIANCES	NONE/NOT INCLUDED	WORKING	NOT WORKING	DO NOT KNOW
Built-in Vacuum System				
Clothes Dryer				
Clothes Washer				
Dishwasher				
Disposal				
Freezer				
Gas Grill				
Hood				
Microwave Oven				
Oven				
Range				
Refrigerator				
Room Air Conditioner				
T.V. Antenna/Dish				
Trash Compactor				

b. ELECTRICAL SYSTEM				
Air Purifier				
Burglar Alarm				
Ceiling Fan				
Garage Door Opener/Control(s)				
Inside Telephone Wiring and Blocks/Jacks				
Intercom				
Light Fixtures				
Sauna				
Smoke/Fire Alarm				
Switches & Outlets				
Telephone Instruments				
Vent Fan				
220 Volt Service				

c. HEATING AND COOLING SYSTEM				
Attic Fan				
Central Air Conditioning				
Evaporative Cooler				
Fireplace				
Fireplace Insert				
Furnace/Heat-Electric				
Furnace/Heat-Gas				
Humidifier				
Propane Tank				
Solar House-Heating				
Woodburning Stove				

d. WATER SYSTEMS				
Cistern				
Hot Tub				
Plumbing				
Pool				
Septic/Leaching Field				
Sump Pump				
Underground Sprinkler				
Water Heater/Electric				
Water Heater/Gas				
Water Heater/Solar				
Water Purifier				
Water Softener				
Well				

2. ROOF:

Age (if known): _____ Years	YES	NO	DO NOT KNOW
a. Does the roof leak?			
b. Is there present damage to the roof?			
c. Is the roof under warranty?			
d. Is warranty transferable?			
e. Expiration date of warranty:			

3. HAZARDOUS CONDITIONS:

Are there any existing hazardous conditions on the property, such as methane gas, lead paint, radon gas in house or well, radio-active material, landfill, mineshaft, expansive soil, toxic materials, urea-formaldehyde foam insulation or asbestos insulation? Explain under additional comments.			

4. OTHER DISCLOSURES:

a. Are the improvements connected to public water system?			
b. Are the improvements connected to public sewer system?			
c. Are the improvements connected to private/community water system?			
d. Are the improvements connected to private/community sewer system?			
e. Do improvements have aluminum wiring?			
f. Are any trees or shrubs diseased or dead?			
g. Are there any encroachments?			
h. Are there any violations of zoning, building code, or restrictive covenants?			
i. Is the present use a non-conforming use?			
j. Have you received any notices by any governmental or quasi-governmental agency affecting the property?			
k. Are there any structural problems with the improvements?			
l. Have any substantial additions or alterations been made without a required building permit?			
m. Are there moisture and/or water problems in basement or crawl space?			
n. Is there any damage due to wind, fire, flood, termites or rodents?			
o. When was fireplace/wood stove, chimney/flue last cleaned? Date:			

5. ADDITIONAL COMMENTS AND/OR EXPLANATIONS: (Use additional pages if necessary)

The information contained in this Disclosure has been furnished by the Seller, who certifies to the truth thereof based on the Seller's **CURRENT ACTUAL KNOWLEDGE.** Any important changes will be disclosed by Seller to Purchaser prior to closing. Seller hereby receipts for a copy of this Disclosure.

Purchaser hereby receipts for a copy of this Disclosure.

Seller _____ Date _____

Purchaser _____ Date _____

Seller _____ Date _____

Purchaser _____ Date _____

Seller and Purchaser understand that _____ (Broker's Firm Name)
in no way warrants or guarantees the above information on the property. Property inspection reports and/or home protection plans may be purchased.

SELLER'S PROPERTY DISCLOSURE

Internal Office Stamps

As our offices become more and more hectic and busy, there is a need to have easy access to standard stamps for certain document tracking tasks. With the advent of the "self inking" stamp, the old stamp ink pad is no longer a deterrent to this type of simple easy-to-implement risk management system. It also lightens the load on the person at the front desk trying to deal with what is hopefully a busy and intense situation with a degree of consistent professionalism. Some of these stamps are as follows:

For rough drafts, not
intended to be executed: **DRAFT ONLY—DO NOT EXECUTE**

To differentiate between a
copy of an original and
a copy of a FAX: **COPY OF FAX—NOT OF AN ORIGINAL**

For an office's internal records, to determine and utilize in the future as proof, indicating when documents were mailed or delivered to a client, customer or third party:

A Copy of the document consisting of _____ pages was
☐ Mailed   ☐ Hand Delivered to:

☐ Client: _____
☐ Customer: _____
☐ Lender: _____
☐ Escrow: _____
☐ Title Co: _____
☐ Attorney: _____

By: _____ **on** _____ **19**____
    (initial)   **(date)**

Another form:

COPY, consisting of _____ **pages,**

mailed to: _____

on _____ **19**____ **by:** _____

Open House Agency Disclosure

When do you have to give the purchaser or prospective purchaser a disclosure regarding your role as the seller's agent at an open house? The rules and laws across the country and in various offices vary widely. The courts of different jurisdictions will someday have to start determining what is timely and adequate. Some states have statutes trying to set standards.

This idea represents a supplement to existing statutes, court cases, regulations and office policy in effect or proposed. It is just another little advantage for the alert and risk-conscious agent and broker who is trying to eliminate or alleviate the potential risk and still concentrate on selling real estate and holding open houses. The common question is: "When should I give the disclosure without scaring away the buyer?"

Place a sign on the door of an open house through which all prospective purchasers must pass that reads:

JONES REALTY AND MARY JONES
as exclusive agents for
JOHNSON BUILDERS

Welcome you to our Open House

An alternative is to place a placard at the top of the sign-in register where you make sure all prospective purchasers sign in before they discuss their real estate needs with you. The notation reads:

JONES REALTY AND MARY JONES
as exclusive agents for
ALEXANDER AND MONICA SELLER

Welcome you to our Open House

While this may not suffice for a required disclosure to be executed by a prospective purchaser, which may be required by state or regulatory law, it will start the disclosure process moving and begin to protect you when the prospective purchaser begins to disclose their innermost thoughts and desires.

The Postcard

Easy, fast, inexpensive, simple and effective. Mailing a postcard to a client or customer can be the best way to update someone on the process of a certain task—such as the sale of their home. This system reduces confusion, discourages unwanted calls from other agents, documents the status of a situation, all without the need for a letter. A series of postcards can be preprinted with a form or with blanks for the various needs that arise. Postcards can even be ordered with NCR carbon paper so that the sending office retains a copy of the information.

Informed people who "know what's going on" are a lot less likely to call their agent and take up valuable time. In addition they are not feeling neglected and thinking about starting to fuss or sue. Think about having the cards printed on double length stock so that they can be folded over and stapled, thereby keeping the information confidential as they are mailed to the addressee.

After Showings

The postcard is a great substitute for a phone call to each seller after each showing. Or after a week of showings, how about sending a little postcard?

This doubles as a great way to encourage someone to improve the way their home shows. Note the post card below with suggestions. There is no need to check any particular suggestion, hence the room for a congratulatory note. The seller will read all the items indicated, regardless of the fact that you have not checked a particular item. The seller will think about each item and the effect that it could have upon the sale of the home. This way you can present the news without having to feel as if you are being critical.

The "official use" boxes on the next page are used as follows:

official use only

☐ card sent   initials of the person sending this card

☐ sub ☐ bb   check for subagent or buyer broker (agent)

Showing Report

Date(s) Shown: _____

official use only

[___] card sent

☐ sub   ☐ bb

Comments:

Your home was shown on the above dates. These are the comments that we received. We thought that you would like to know. Thank you for selecting us as your agents to market your home. Please call if you would like more detail.

© 1990 Real Law Books, Inc.   P.O.Box 3113   Boulder, CO 80307   All Rights Reserved

Showing Report/Suggestions

Date(s) Shown: _____

official use only

[___] card sent

☐ sub   ☐ bb

Comments:

Suggestions to enhance future showings:

☐ Paint the exterior   ☐ Paint the interior
☐ Have the carpets cleaned   ☐ Remove animals early
☐ Children visit friends   ☐ Tenant incentives
☐ Remove/store some personal items—home seems larger
☐ None—Your home looks great
☐ _____
☐ Please call me at 494-6661 when you can.

Your home was shown on the above dates. These are the comments that we received. We thought that you would like to know.

I have checked some suggestions that might assist us in showing your home in the future. Please review them and I will contact you soon so that we can plan for future showings. Thank you for selecting us as your agents to market your home. Please call if you would like more detail.

© 1990 Real Law Books, Inc.   P.O.Box 3113   Boulder, CO 80307   All Rights Reserved

Agency Confirmation Card

Date: _____ 19_____   Call taken by: _____

Property Address: _____

Agent: _____   Other Office: _____

Phone: (_____) _____   _____

    Thank you for displaying an interest in our listing. This is to confirm that you and your brokerage office are acting as:

☐ our subagents   ☐ agents for the buyer

and that you will receive, as your sole compensation as the result of the sale of this property, upon sale, closing and payment to this office of the gross commission by the seller:

      ☐ _____% of the gross selling price   ☐ $_____._____

☐ Showing appointment was made by: _____

    showing on _____ 19_____ at _____:_____ a.m. p.m.

All offers to purchase **must** be accompanied by:

☐ a copy of the Seller's Property Statement initialed by the purchaser.
☐ a properly executed Agency Disclosure form.

    Thank you for assisting us with the sale of this property.

Agency Confirmation

Date: _____ 19_____   Call taken by: _____

Property Address: _____

Thank you for your telephone call today and your interest in our client's property.

Agent: _____   Other Office: _____

Phone: (_____) _____   _____

This is to confirm that you and your brokerage office are acting as:

☐ our subagents   ☐ agents for the buyer

and that you will receive, as a result of the sale of this property

☐ as your sole compensation   ☐ as part of your compensation
☐ no compensation; you are being paid by your client, the buyer,

a commission calculated as follows:

☐ _____% of the gross selling price   ☐ $_____._____

payable by this firm as follows:

☐ in cash at closing   ☐ when we receive payment from the seller

We require that all offers to purchase **must** be accompanied by:

☐ a copy of the Seller's Property Statement initialed by the purchaser.
☐ a properly executed Agency Disclosure form.

Showing appointment was made by: _____

for a showing on _____19_____ at _____:_____ a.m. p.m.

Thank you for assisting us with the sale of this property.

Standard Disclosure Authorization

As the agents employed to assist you in the sale of your property, we often receive inquiries from other brokers, either acting as either our sub-agents or as representatives of a purchaser, buyer's agents, or from prospective purchasers themselves requesting information about you as the seller that we feel you might find confidential. In order to respond to those inquiries we need direction from you. For each item please indicate the response that you wish us to give to an inquiry.

Information Requested	Yes	No	No Comment	Comments
Death in the house	_____	_____	_____	_____
Ghosts in the house	_____	_____	_____	_____
Violent crime on the property	_____	_____	_____	_____
AIDS patients	_____	_____	_____	_____
Transfer pending	_____	_____	_____	_____
Home buyout pending	_____	_____	_____	_____
Bankruptcy pending	_____	_____	_____	_____
Divorce pending	_____	_____	_____	_____

In our advertising we wish direction so that we can use words or phrases that you approve of. For each of the following, please indicate the words or phrases that we are authorized to utilize in our advertising, MLS, newspaper, marketing breakfasts, property exchange sessions, to name a few:

☐ **OK to use**   ☐ **Do not use**   **"Seller motivated to sell"**
☐ **OK to use**   ☐ **Do not use**   **"Bring any offer"**
☐ **OK to use**   ☐ **Do not use**   **"Transferred"**
☐ **OK to use**   ☐ **Do not use**   **"Foreclosure"**
☐ **OK to use**   ☐ **Do not use**
☐ **OK to use**   ☐ **Do not use**
☐ **OK to use**   ☐ **Do not use**

Thank you for your direction. As part of our advertising program, we will periodically send you copies of the advertising that we are submitting for your benefit. Please review it and inform us if it is not as you desire. Unless we hear to the contrary, we will assume that the advertising that we send to you is proper and authorized on your behalf.

Seller: _____ _____
(signature)   (date)

Seller: _____ _____
(signature)   (date)

Contract Language

So many people at live programs have asked that this language be made available in the book that I have included it in this appendix. Although care is taken in this book not to suggest contract language for many reasons, not the least of which is the diverse contract formats in the different states and locations across the country, the following language is provided for your revision and use:

Short Payoff

Seller's obligations under this contract are expressly conditional upon the lender holding the note secured by the first lien (deed of trust or mortgage as your state may be) upon the property agreeing in written form, on or before _____ 19_____, to accept the net proceeds (sales price less commission, new loan points, tax prorations and other contract obligations and customary closing items) in full satisfaction of the indicated indebtedness.

The key items to look for are: the identity or reference to the lender, net proceeds, and full satisfaction of the debt.

Comparable Properties

Many brokers use "comps" to help in the listing and sale process. Leaving aside the discussion of when and to whom should comparable property information be shown, there is a need to explain exactly what a "comp" is and is not. It is not universal in every state, as some states actually do have all sold properties, plus those reported through the MLS system and the records of the clerk and recorder, available online and accessible with a computer. In addition, we have all worked to supply different parties with comparable sold properties which enhance our opinion of the relative value of the property. This little inclusion may help:

The properties listed herein are an excerpt of the properties that have sold in this area compiled from the records of the Multiple Listing Service and do not necessarily represent all of the property sold through the MLS or otherwise in this particular price, location and market. They are offered as a guide only.

While I know of no reason to doubt the authenticity of these selected comparable properties, I cannot be responsible for their selection nor for the information that is indicated therein.

The seller's specific authorization to show listed and sold "comps" to the buyer is extremely valuable and should be included in the listing agreement.

I hereby authorize you to provide data about comparable listed and sold properties available through the MLS system to prospective purchasers in order to assist them in valuing my property.

Dual Agency Disclosure

While dual agency is authorized in some states by statute and therefore many people think it is "OK" to do just about anything, the concept is still one where broker liability is not only present but potentially devastating. The rule we follow is "the first one to sue gets most of the money and the second one gets the rest." Nevertheless I am repeatedly asked for a series of contract paragraphs that will help with the problem.

The following wording is not recommended. Consult with a local attorney before utilizing any language regarding dual agency or simultaneous agency.

First you must insert language in the listing contract explaining to the seller what may occur. Similar language will also have to be placed in a letter or addendum to the Exclusive Buyer Agency or other Buyer Agency or Buyer Broker Agreement. This language must take into account that you will learn secrets about the buyer that you will not be disclosing to the seller and that you may disclose secrets to the buyer that you have learned from the seller. A few of the obvious ones include the price that the seller needs, the amount the buyer will pay, the number of points that either party will pay, the interest rate or other terms on ownercarry or "creative" financing, the financial status of either party, and their relative urgency to buy or sell. A plain language paragraph follows:

The listing broker and its agents, in addition to offering representation of sellers such as yourselves, also offers representation to purchasers. This may include other sellers who have listed their property with this office, sellers who have listed their property with other members of the MLS service and purchasers who are simply seeking housing.

It is possible that we will be placed in a position of representing you as a seller and either myself or another agent in the office representing the purchaser for this property. In that event, you understand that we are authorized to disclose to the purchaser any information, personal or with regard to the property, that you have disclosed to us in confidence or otherwise. Please refrain from providing us with such information or any other information that you do not wish a prospective purchaser to know.

*In the reverse, we may have learned information about the pro-
spective purchaser that we do not disclose to you. The retention
of this information may or may not be important to you and you
understand that you cannot hold us responsible for the failure to
disclose such information.*

In most states, the broker is the listing entity acting through agents,
salespersons or brokers in a salesperson's capacity and, as such, is personally
the agent for each seller and purchaser. Absent a regulation or statute to the
contrary, even though one salesperson may "have the purchaser" and the
other "has the listing", the broker "has them both."

Goodbye and Good Luck!

I have been pleased to have you join me on this passage down *The Paper Trail* and wish you the best of prosperity, clarity, and the resulting happiness that comes from the inner knowledge that you are doing a professional job of assisting people with their most basic of needs, shelter. If you have questions or comments, please feel free to drop me a letter. I want to continue making this guide as useful a tool as I possibly can, and I would value your thoughts as you modify and apply these ideas and methods in the course of your own work.

The Author

Oliver E. Frascona is a Colorado native, born and raised in Boulder, Colorado. He did his undergraduate work at the University of Colorado, graduating as a Bachelor of Science in business with an emphasis in finance and real estate.

Mr. Frascona's mother, Jean Helen Ezard, an English barrister, and his father, Joseph L. Frascona, a professor, author and attorney, instilled in him a strong desire to become an attorney. After serving as an officer in the United States Navy Reserve, he returned to Colorado, became a licensed real estate salesperson and subsequently a broker, attended law school while working as a residential real estate salesman, and graduated with a Doctor of Jurisprudence degree from the University of Denver School of Law in 1974. He began his legal career by practicing real estate and business law. A member of the Colorado Association of Realtors®, he has been a licensed Colorado real estate broker since 1972.

A partner in the law firm of Frascona, Joiner and Smittkamp, Mr. Frascona limits his personal practice to real estate, business and association law. He is currently a Certified Advanced Law Instructor for the Colorado Association of Realtors®, the attorney for twelve local boards of Realtors, three metro area boards and nine rural boards, is a member of the Colorado Association of Certified Closers and the attorney for many real estate companies, large and small. He is also the attorney for first and second mortgage lenders, banks and bankers, savings and loan associations, private developers, and numerous private individuals.

A much sought after speaker, he lectures frequently across the country for numerous State Associations and local Boards, the memberships of large and small brokerage concerns, and various other groups, including the National Association of Realtors® on topics relating to real estate, business and association law. A member of the Real Estate Educators Association and holding the Designated Real Estate Instructor (DREI) designation, he has had many of his programs certified for continuing education credit.

As an active investor for his personal account, Mr. Frascona has the opportunity to, and regularly does, utilize the services of real estate professionals for the purchase, sale, and management of real estate on behalf of his clients and himself. He is the author of other manuals for the real estate professional and considers his mission as a lawyer to be that of a deal maker rather than a deal breaker. In this regard, he appreciates, recommends, and frequently utilizes the services of good real estate brokers.

REAL LAW BOOKS, INC.

Post Office Box 3113 Boulder, Colorado 80307-3113

Telephone 303-494-6661

RISK REDUCTION SERIES®

_____ **Books,** *The Paper Trail* by Oliver E. Frascona   @ **35.00** $_____.__

_____ **Computer Diskettes**—sample letters and forms
from the book   @ **69.95** $_____.__

Computer: _____ IBM®& Compatibles **or**
_____ Macintosh®

Wordprocessor: _____ ASCII (all word processors) **or**
_____ WordPerfect®

Diskette Size: _____ 5 ¹/₄" **or** _____ 3 ¹/₂"

_____ **Audio Cassette Libraries** (6 tapes)
"Liability Reduction Techniques"   @ **69.95** $_____.__

_____ **Video Tape Libraries** (4 VHS tapes)
"Liability Reduction Techniques"   @ **189.95** $_____.__

Colorado residents add 6.23% sales tax $_____.__

Mail order postage and handling $___**3.00**__

(Please print or attach your business card)   **Total Order $**_____.__

Name:_____   ___ Check ___Cash

Company: _____   ___MC ___Visa ___ Amex

Address: _____ Card No: _____-_____-_____-_____

City:_____ State:_____ Zip:_____ Exp. Date:_____
Charge this purchase to my account

Signature: _____ Phone: (____)_____

For faster service,
Call: **(303) 494-6661**

BUSINESS REPLY MAIL
FIRST CLASS   PERMIT NO. 382   BOULDER, CO

POSTAGE WILL BE PAID BY ADDRESSEE

Real Law Books, Inc.
P.O. Box 3113
Boulder, CO 80307-9975

FOLD HERE

TAPE EDGES